THE TROJAN HORSE

THE FALL OF TROY

A GREEK MYTH

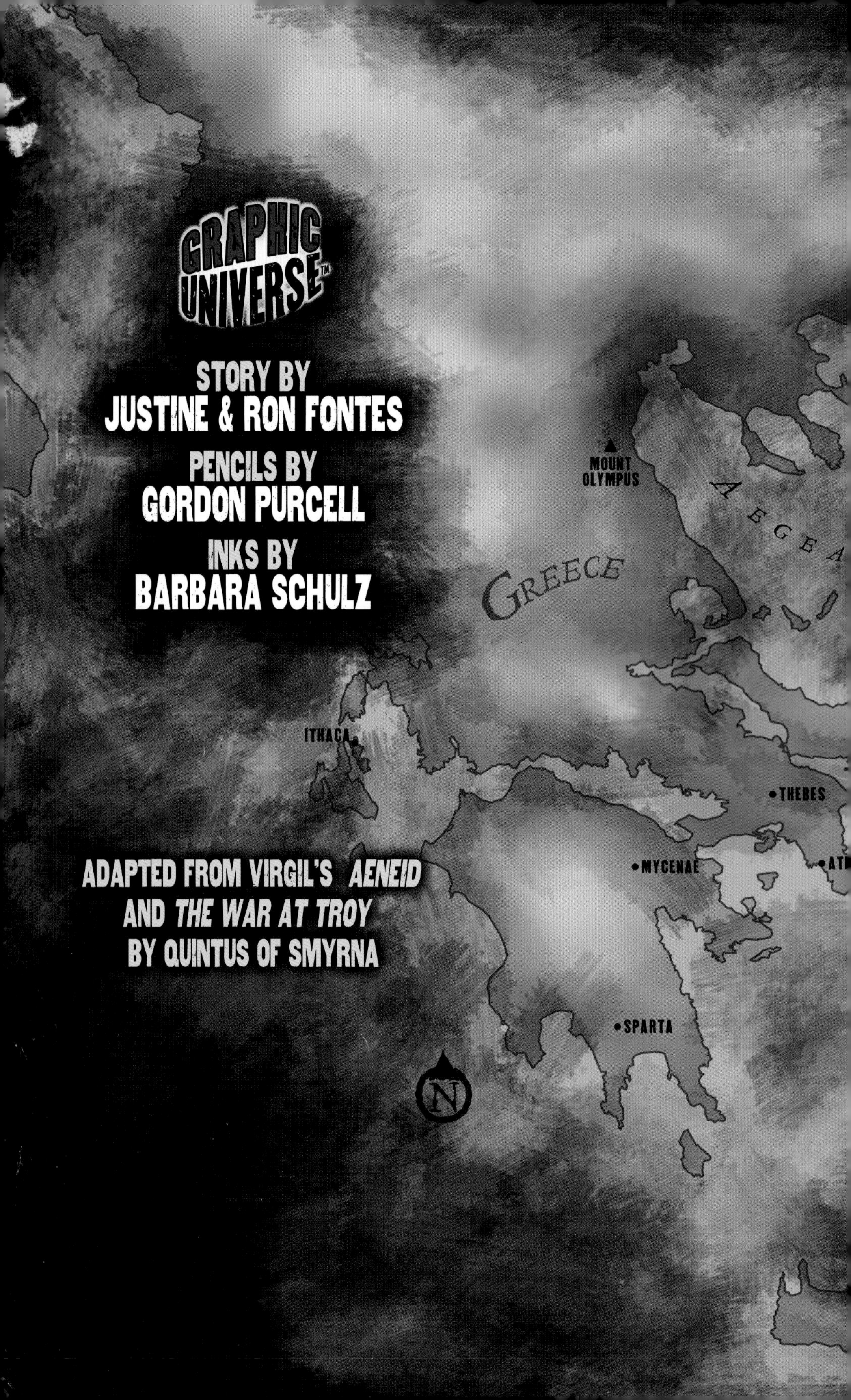

MOUNT OLYMPUS
GREECE
ITHACA
THEBES
MYCENAE
SPARTA
N

GRAPHIC UNIVERSE™

STORY BY
JUSTINE & RON FONTES
PENCILS BY
GORDON PURCELL
INKS BY
BARBARA SCHULZ

ADAPTED FROM VIRGIL'S *AENEID*
AND *THE WAR AT TROY*
BY QUINTUS OF SMYRNA

THE TROJAN HORSE

THE FALL OF TROY

A GREEK MYTH

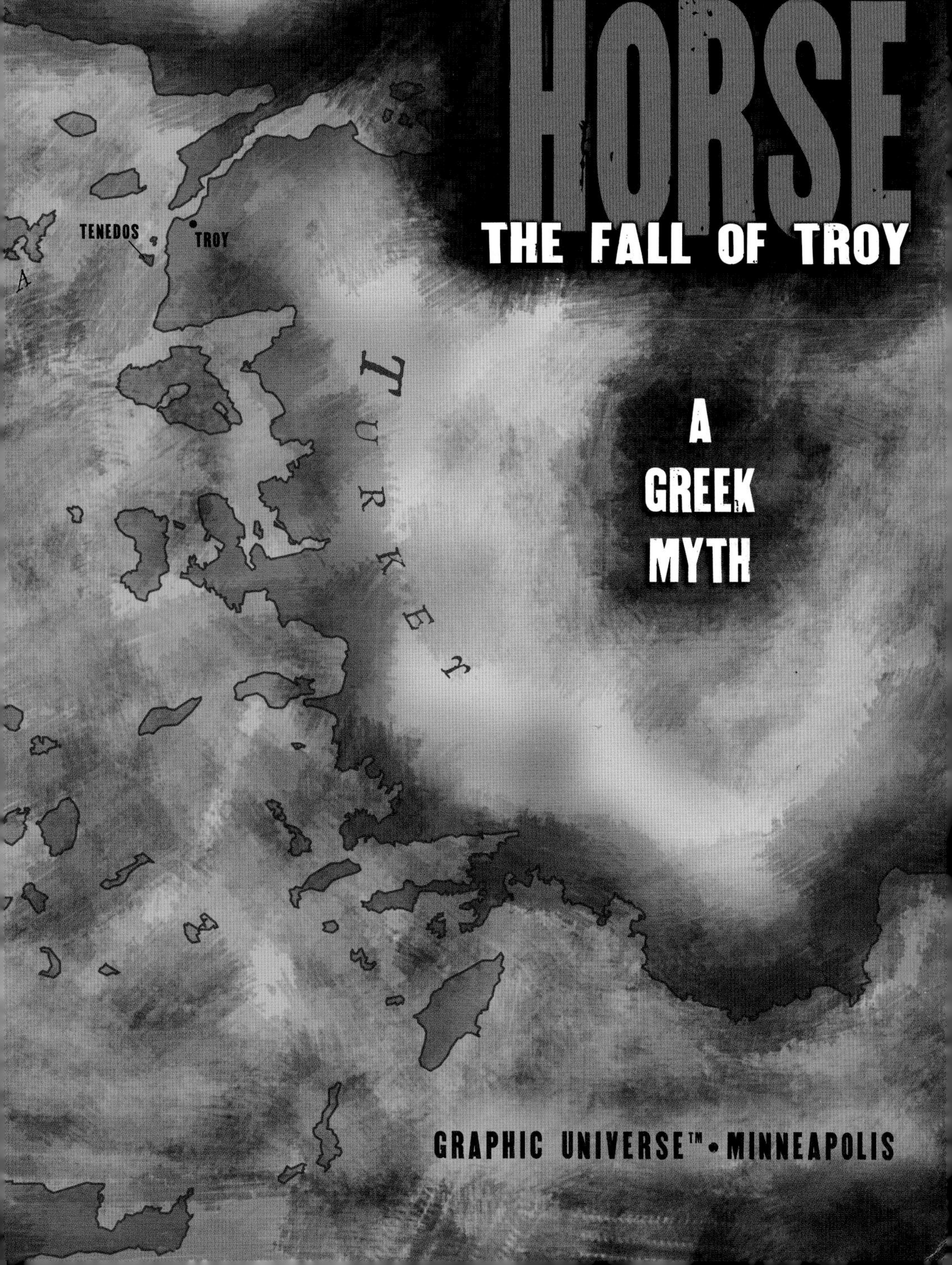
TENEDOS
TROY
TURKEY

GRAPHIC UNIVERSE™ • MINNEAPOLIS

ANCIENT LEGENDS OF A WAR BETWEEN THE GREEK CITY STATES AND TROY THAT MAY HAVE TAKEN PLACE AROUND 1200 B.C. WERE GATHERED INTO GREAT EPIC POEMS BY WRITERS OF LATER TIMES. THE GREEK POET HOMER WROTE THE ILIAD ABOUT 700-800 B.C. IT TELLS OF THE GREEK HEROES, PARTICULARLY ACHILLES, AS THEY FOUGHT AGAINST TROY TO RECLAIM HELEN, WIFE OF MENELAUS, KING OF SPARTA. THE STORY OF THE FALL OF TROY AND OF THE HORSE LEFT BEHIND BY THE GREEKS APPEARS IN THE AENEID, WRITTEN BY THE ROMAN POET VIRGIL BETWEEN 42 AND 35 B.C. RON & JUSTINE FONTES HAVE BASED THEIR RETELLING ON THESE SOURCES AND ON THE WAR AT TROY, WRITTEN BY GREEK POET QUINTUS OF SMYRNA AROUND A.D. 375.

STORY BY JUSTINE & RON FONTES

PENCILS BY GORDON PURCELL
INKS BY BARBARA SCHULZ

COLORING BY HI-FI DESIGN

LETTERING BY BILL HAUSER

Copyright © 2007 by Lerner Publishing Group, Inc.

Graphic Universe ™ is a trademark of Lerner Publishing Group, Inc.

Graphic Universe ™
A division of Lerner Publishing Group, Inc.
241 First Avenue North
Minneapolis, MN 55401 U.S.A.

Website address: www.lernerbooks.com

Library of Congress Cataloging-in-Publication Data

Fontes, Justine.
    The Trojan horse: the fall of Troy / by Justine & Ron Fontes; adapted from Virgil's Aeneid and The war at troy by Quintus of Smyrna; illustrations by Gordon Purcell.
       p.   cm. — (Graphic myths and legends)
    Includes bibliographical references and index.
    ISBN-13: 978-0-8225-3085-5 (lib. bdg. : alk. paper)
    ISBN-10: 0-8225-3085-6 (lib. bdg. : alk. paper)
       1. Trojan War—Comic books, strips, etc.
    2. Graphic novels. I. Fontes, Justine. II. Purcell, Gordon. III. Virgil Aeneis. IV. Quintus, Smyrnaeus, 4th cent. Posthomerica. V. Title. VI. Series: Graphic Myths and Legends (Minneapolis, Minn.)
    BL793.T7F66 2007
    741.5'673—dc22   2005023776

Manufactured in the United States of America
5 - DP - 8/20/09

TABLE OF CONTENTS

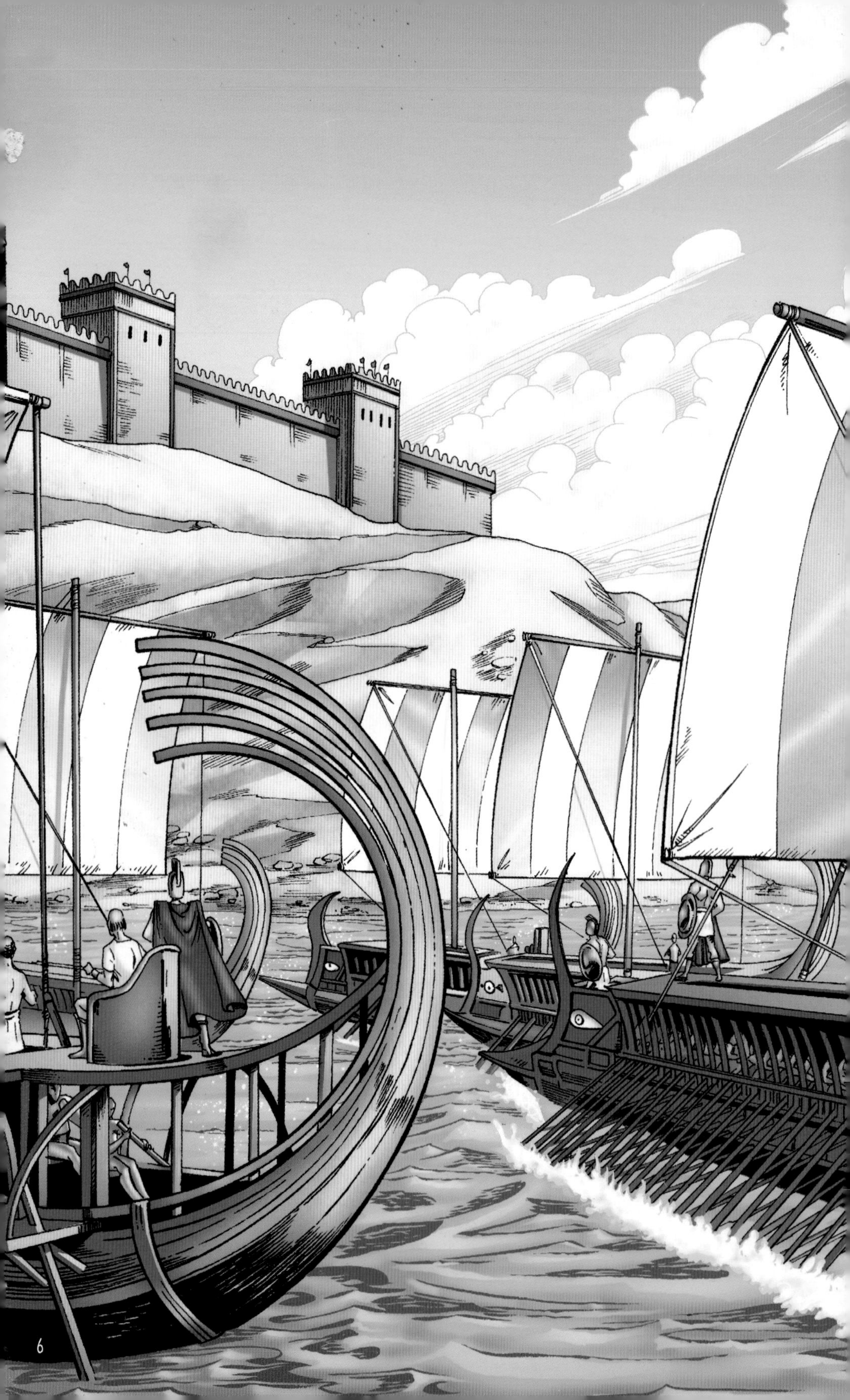

A ROTTEN APPLE

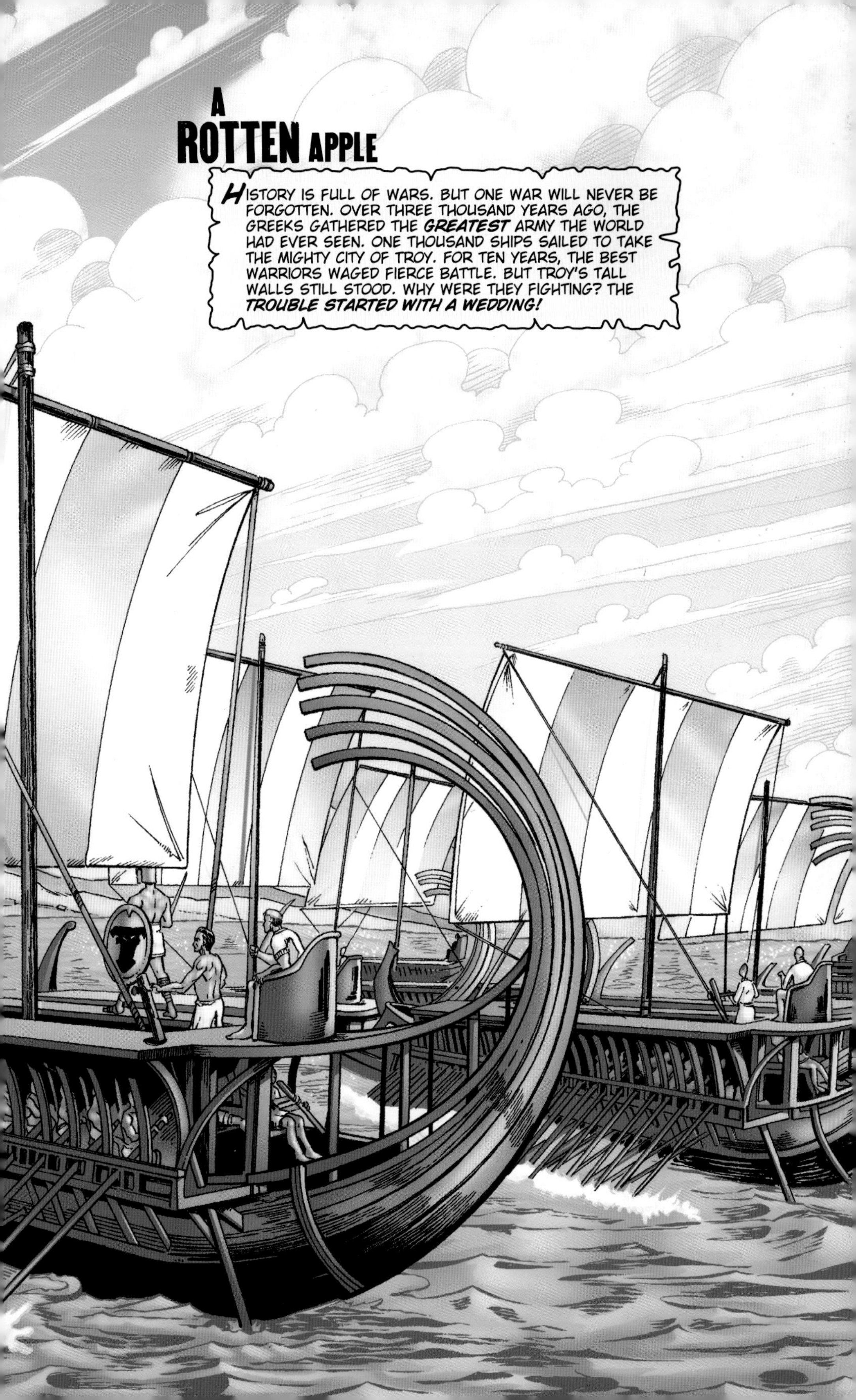
HISTORY IS FULL OF WARS. BUT ONE WAR WILL NEVER BE FORGOTTEN. OVER THREE THOUSAND YEARS AGO, THE GREEKS GATHERED THE ***GREATEST*** ARMY THE WORLD HAD EVER SEEN. ONE THOUSAND SHIPS SAILED TO TAKE THE MIGHTY CITY OF TROY. FOR TEN YEARS, THE BEST WARRIORS WAGED FIERCE BATTLE. BUT TROY'S TALL WALLS STILL STOOD. WHY WERE THEY FIGHTING? THE ***TROUBLE STARTED WITH A WEDDING!***

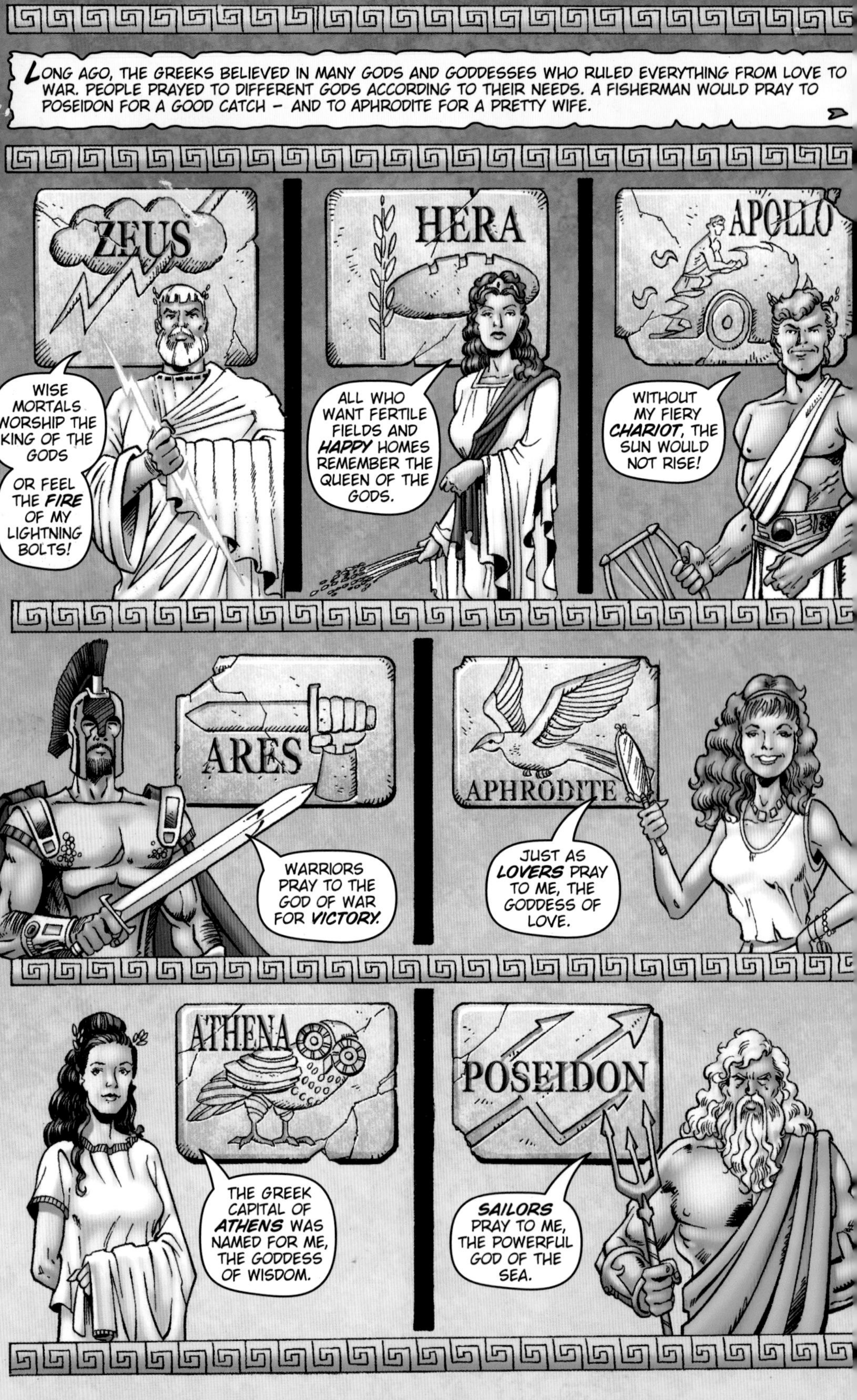
LONG AGO, THE GREEKS BELIEVED IN MANY GODS AND GODDESSES WHO RULED EVERYTHING FROM LOVE TO WAR. PEOPLE PRAYED TO DIFFERENT GODS ACCORDING TO THEIR NEEDS. A FISHERMAN WOULD PRAY TO POSEIDON FOR A GOOD CATCH – AND TO APHRODITE FOR A PRETTY WIFE.
ZEUS
WISE MORTALS WORSHIP THE KING OF THE GODS
OR FEEL THE FIRE OF MY LIGHTNING BOLTS!
HERA
ALL WHO WANT FERTILE FIELDS AND HAPPY HOMES REMEMBER THE QUEEN OF THE GODS.
APOLLO
WITHOUT MY FIERY CHARIOT, THE SUN WOULD NOT RISE!
ARES
WARRIORS PRAY TO THE GOD OF WAR FOR VICTORY.
APHRODITE
JUST AS LOVERS PRAY TO ME, THE GODDESS OF LOVE.
ATHENA
THE GREEK CAPITAL OF ATHENS WAS NAMED FOR ME, THE GODDESS OF WISDOM.
POSEIDON
SAILORS PRAY TO ME, THE POWERFUL GOD OF THE SEA.

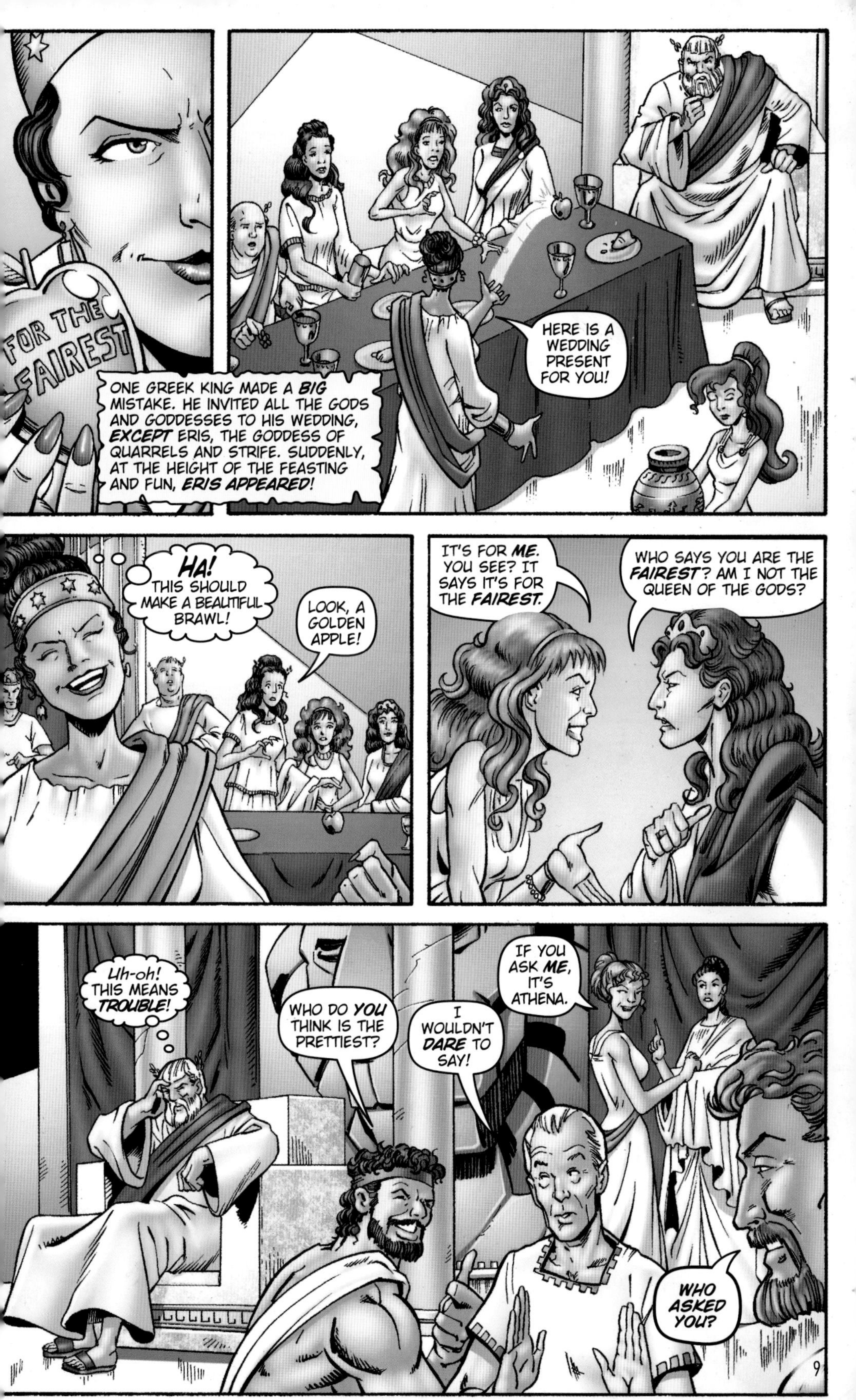
FOR THE FAIREST
ONE GREEK KING MADE A BIG MISTAKE. HE INVITED ALL THE GODS AND GODDESSES TO HIS WEDDING, EXCEPT ERIS, THE GODDESS OF QUARRELS AND STRIFE. SUDDENLY, AT THE HEIGHT OF THE FEASTING AND FUN, ERIS APPEARED!
HERE IS A WEDDING PRESENT FOR YOU!
HA! THIS SHOULD MAKE A BEAUTIFUL BRAWL!
LOOK, A GOLDEN APPLE!
IT'S FOR ME. YOU SEE? IT SAYS IT'S FOR THE FAIREST.
WHO SAYS YOU ARE THE FAIREST? AM I NOT THE QUEEN OF THE GODS?
Uh-oh! THIS MEANS TROUBLE!
WHO DO YOU THINK IS THE PRETTIEST?
I WOULDN'T DARE TO SAY!
IF YOU ASK ME, IT'S ATHENA.
WHO ASKED YOU?

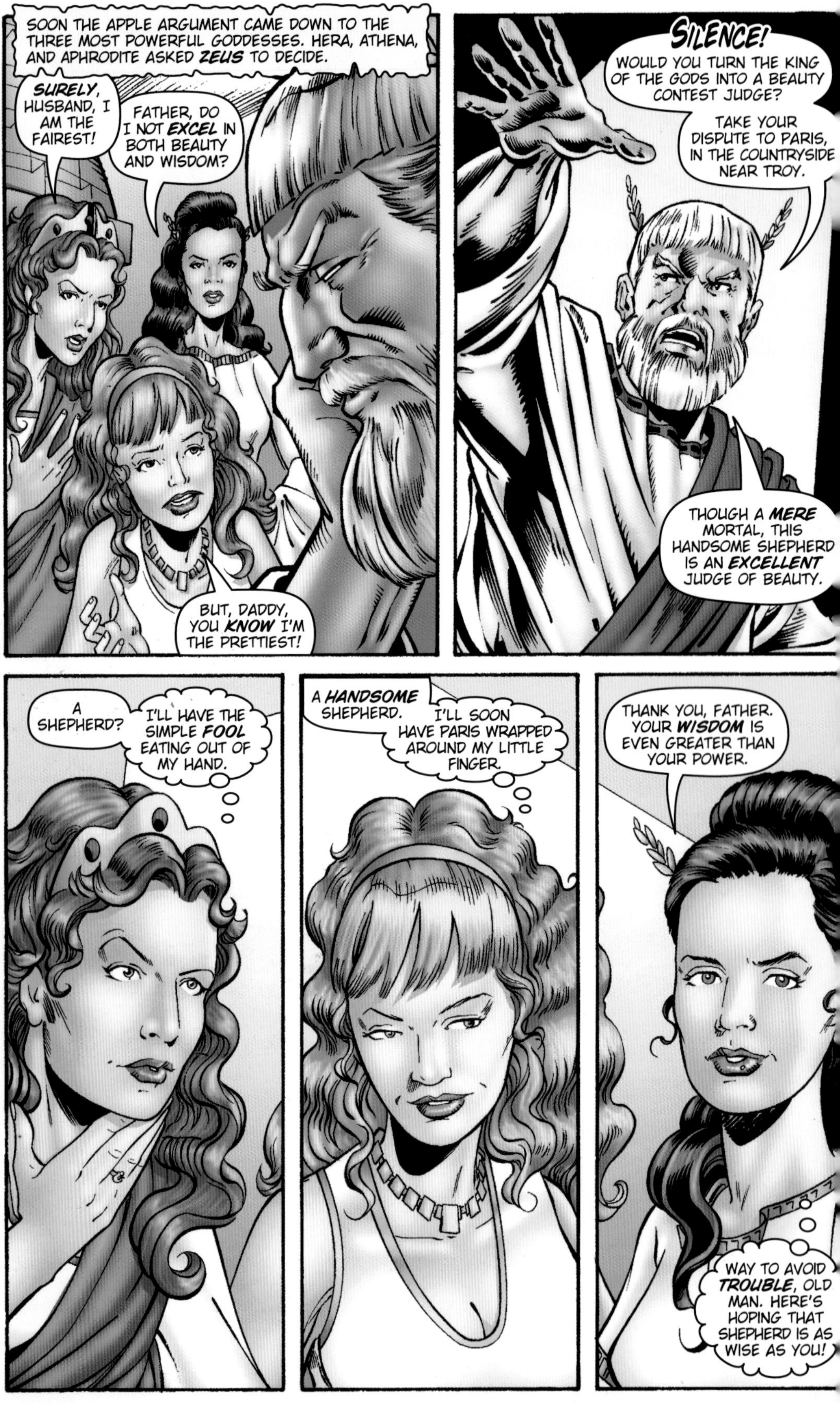
SOON THE APPLE ARGUMENT CAME DOWN TO THE THREE MOST POWERFUL GODDESSES. HERA, ATHENA, AND APHRODITE ASKED ZEUS TO DECIDE.
SURELY, HUSBAND, I AM THE FAIREST!
FATHER, DO I NOT EXCEL IN BOTH BEAUTY AND WISDOM?
BUT, DADDY, YOU KNOW I'M THE PRETTIEST!
SILENCE!
WOULD YOU TURN THE KING OF THE GODS INTO A BEAUTY CONTEST JUDGE?
TAKE YOUR DISPUTE TO PARIS, IN THE COUNTRYSIDE NEAR TROY.
THOUGH A MERE MORTAL, THIS HANDSOME SHEPHERD IS AN EXCELLENT JUDGE OF BEAUTY.
A SHEPHERD?
I'LL HAVE THE SIMPLE FOOL EATING OUT OF MY HAND.
A HANDSOME SHEPHERD.
I'LL SOON HAVE PARIS WRAPPED AROUND MY LITTLE FINGER.
THANK YOU, FATHER. YOUR WISDOM IS EVEN GREATER THAN YOUR POWER.
WAY TO AVOID TROUBLE, OLD MAN. HERE'S HOPING THAT SHEPHERD IS AS WISE AS YOU!

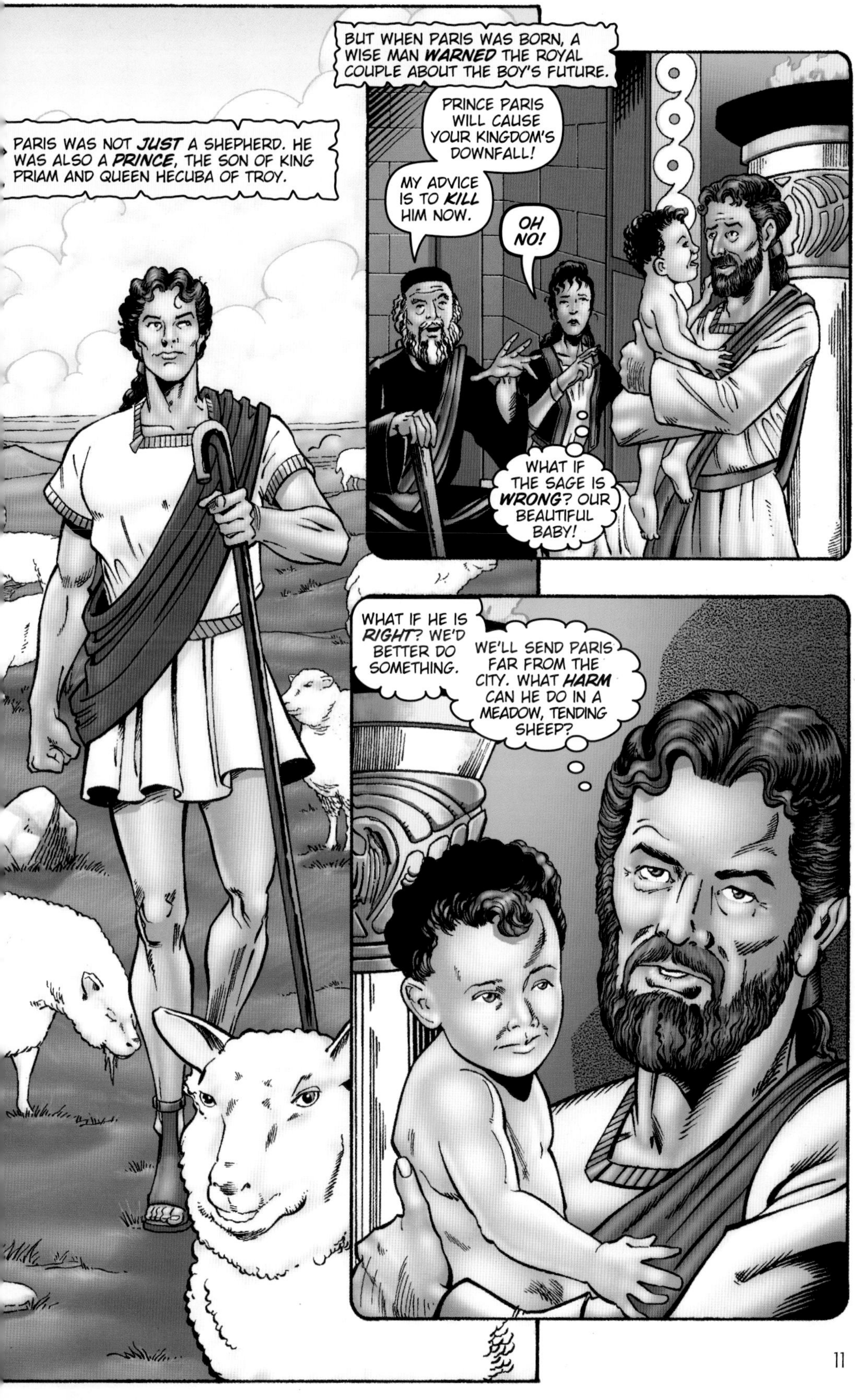
PARIS WAS NOT JUST A SHEPHERD. HE WAS ALSO A PRINCE, THE SON OF KING PRIAM AND QUEEN HECUBA OF TROY.
BUT WHEN PARIS WAS BORN, A WISE MAN WARNED THE ROYAL COUPLE ABOUT THE BOY'S FUTURE.
PRINCE PARIS WILL CAUSE YOUR KINGDOM'S DOWNFALL!
MY ADVICE IS TO KILL HIM NOW.
OH NO!
WHAT IF THE SAGE IS WRONG? OUR BEAUTIFUL BABY!
WHAT IF HE IS RIGHT? WE'D BETTER DO SOMETHING.
WE'LL SEND PARIS FAR FROM THE CITY. WHAT HARM CAN HE DO IN A MEADOW, TENDING SHEEP?

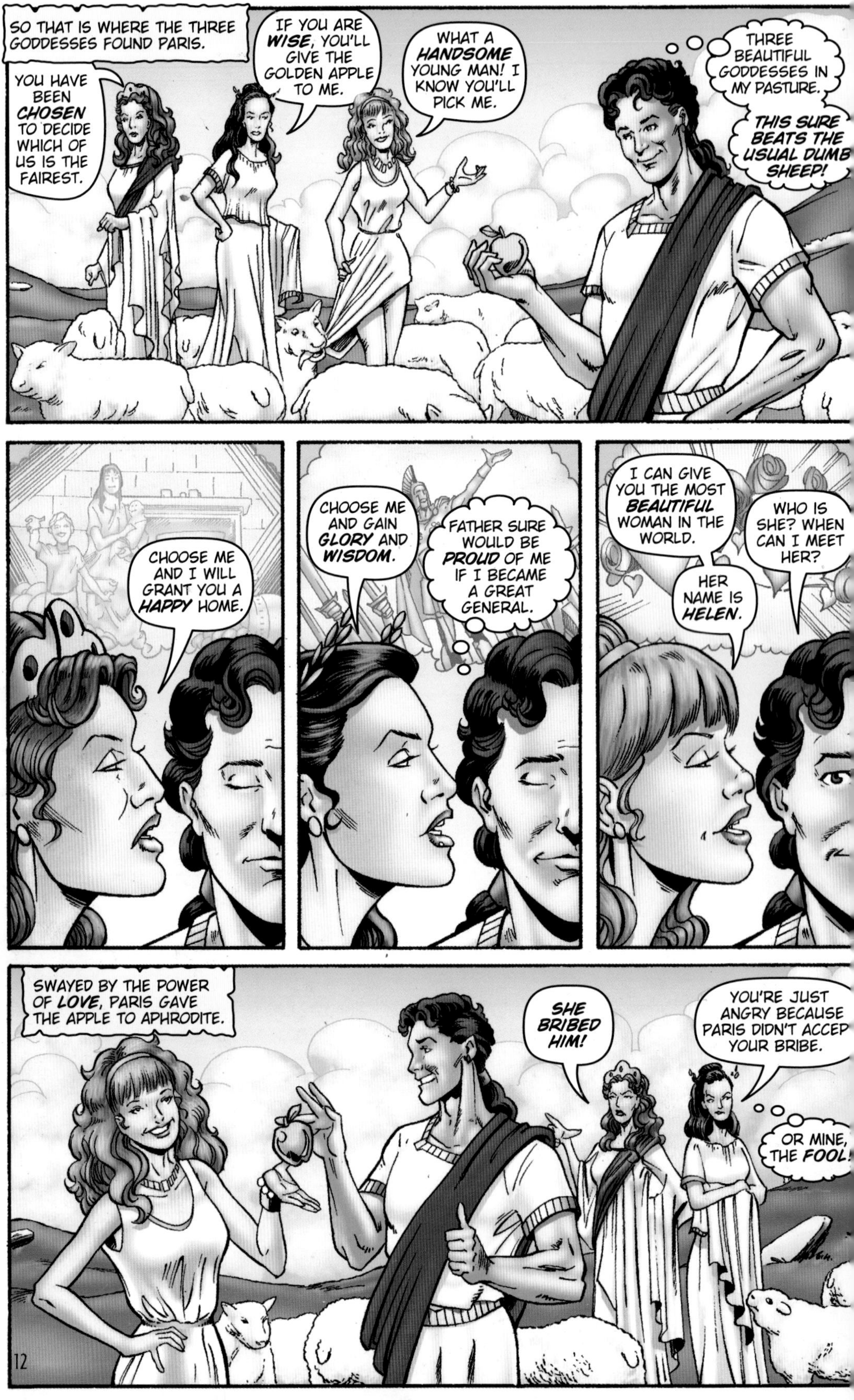
SO THAT IS WHERE THE THREE GODDESSES FOUND PARIS.
YOU HAVE BEEN CHOSEN TO DECIDE WHICH OF US IS THE FAIREST.
IF YOU ARE WISE, YOU'LL GIVE THE GOLDEN APPLE TO ME.
WHAT A HANDSOME YOUNG MAN! I KNOW YOU'LL PICK ME.
THREE BEAUTIFUL GODDESSES IN MY PASTURE.
THIS SURE BEATS THE USUAL DUMB SHEEP!
CHOOSE ME AND I WILL GRANT YOU A HAPPY HOME.
CHOOSE ME AND GAIN GLORY AND WISDOM.
FATHER SURE WOULD BE PROUD OF ME IF I BECAME A GREAT GENERAL.
I CAN GIVE YOU THE MOST BEAUTIFUL WOMAN IN THE WORLD.
WHO IS SHE? WHEN CAN I MEET HER?
HER NAME IS HELEN.
SWAYED BY THE POWER OF LOVE, PARIS GAVE THE APPLE TO APHRODITE.
SHE BRIBED HIM!
YOU'RE JUST ANGRY BECAUSE PARIS DIDN'T ACCEP YOUR BRIBE.
OR MINE, THE FOOL!

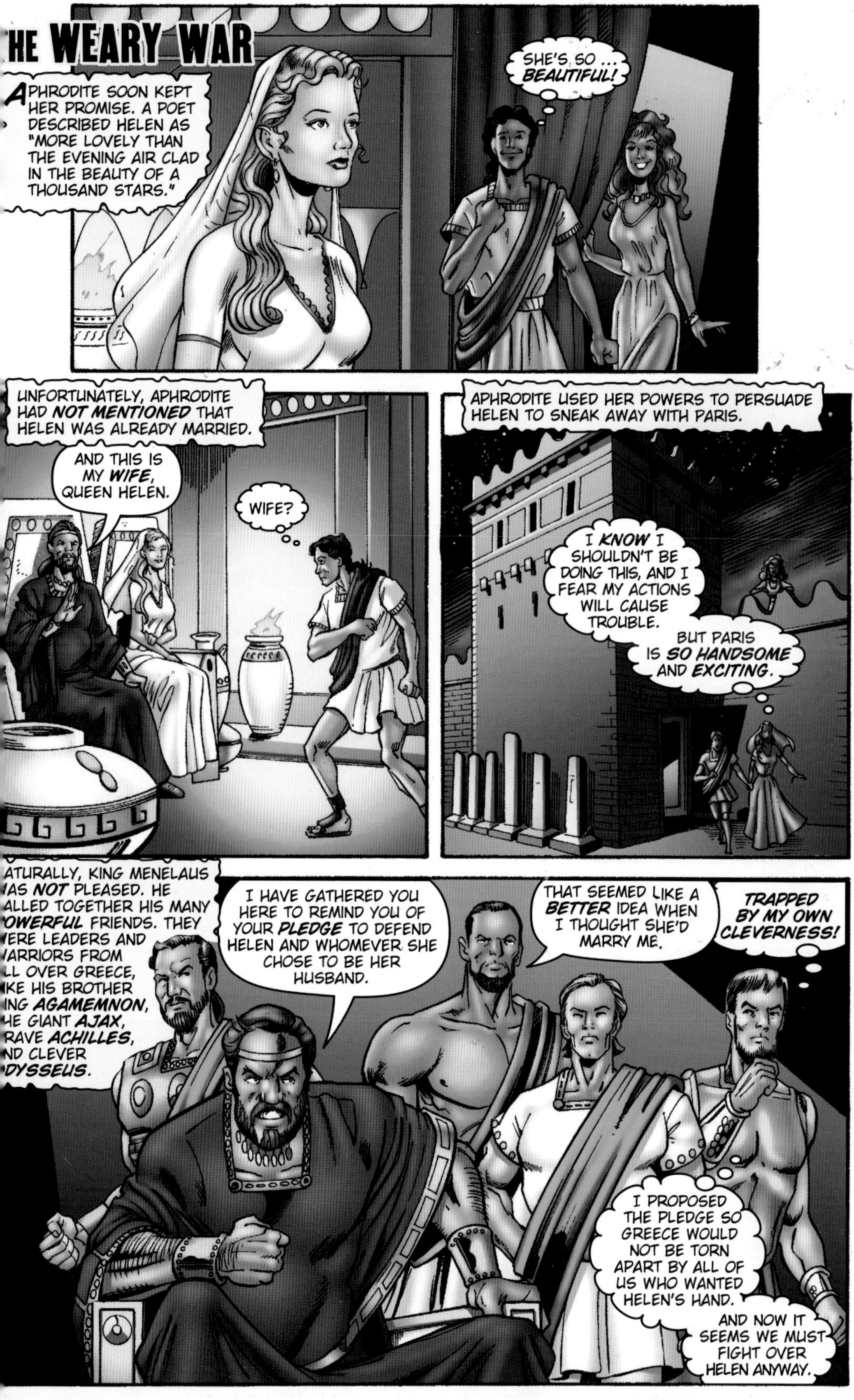
HE WEARY WAR
APHRODITE SOON KEPT HER PROMISE. A POET DESCRIBED HELEN AS "MORE LOVELY THAN THE EVENING AIR CLAD IN THE BEAUTY OF A THOUSAND STARS."
SHE'S SO ... BEAUTIFUL!
UNFORTUNATELY, APHRODITE HAD NOT MENTIONED THAT HELEN WAS ALREADY MARRIED.
AND THIS IS MY WIFE, QUEEN HELEN.
WIFE?
APHRODITE USED HER POWERS TO PERSUADE HELEN TO SNEAK AWAY WITH PARIS.
I KNOW I SHOULDN'T BE DOING THIS, AND I FEAR MY ACTIONS WILL CAUSE TROUBLE.
BUT PARIS IS SO HANDSOME AND EXCITING.
ATURALLY, KING MENELAUS IAS NOT PLEASED. HE ALLED TOGETHER HIS MANY OWERFUL FRIENDS. THEY ERE LEADERS AND ARRIORS FROM LL OVER GREECE, KE HIS BROTHER ING AGAMEMNON, HE GIANT AJAX, RAVE ACHILLES, ND CLEVER DYSSEUS.
I HAVE GATHERED YOU HERE TO REMIND YOU OF YOUR PLEDGE TO DEFEND HELEN AND WHOMEVER SHE CHOSE TO BE HER HUSBAND.
THAT SEEMED LIKE A BETTER IDEA WHEN I THOUGHT SHE'D MARRY ME.
TRAPPED BY MY OWN CLEVERNESS!
I PROPOSED THE PLEDGE SO GREECE WOULD NOT BE TORN APART BY ALL OF US WHO WANTED HELEN'S HAND.
AND NOW IT SEEMS WE MUST FIGHT OVER HELEN ANYWAY.

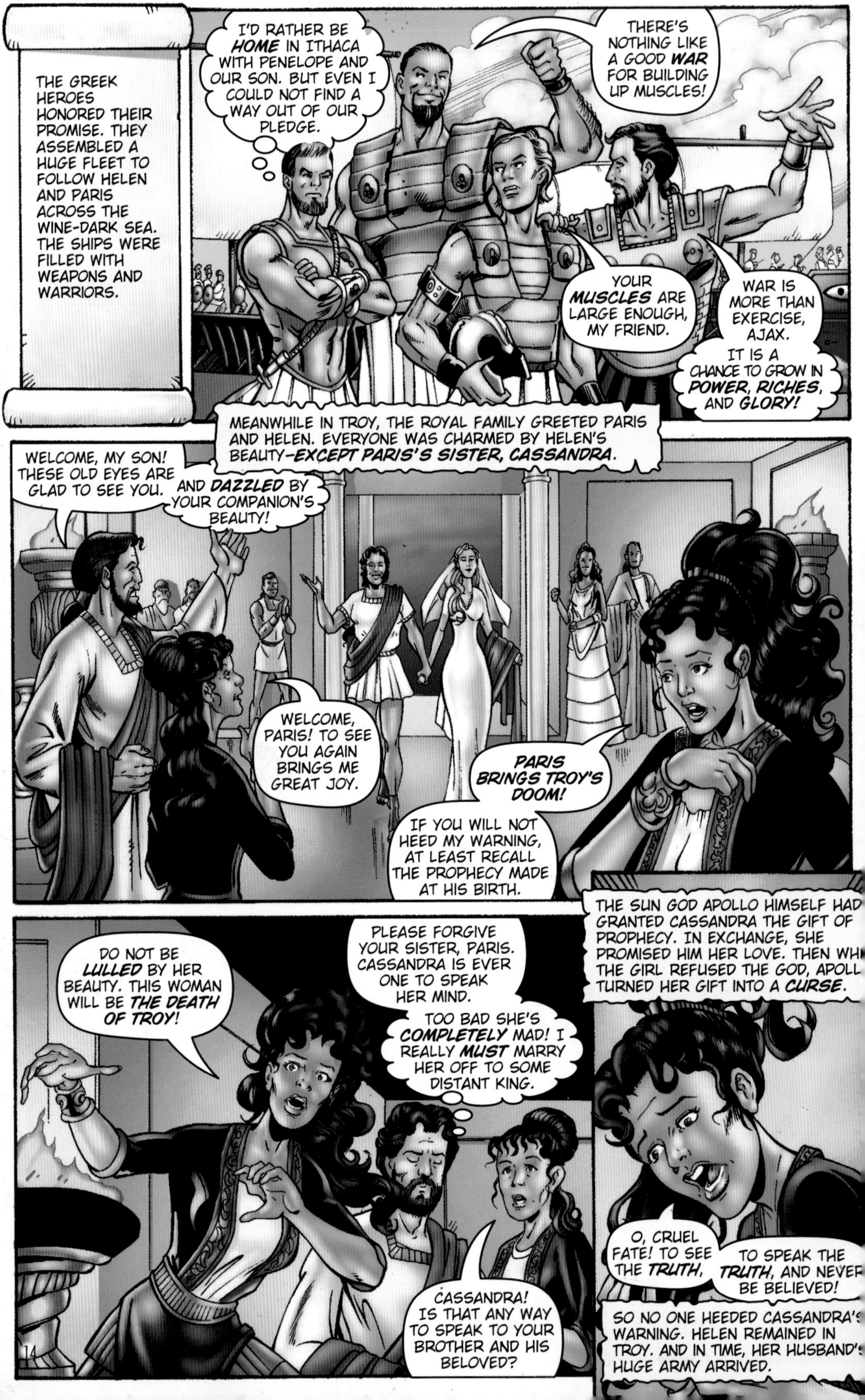

THE GREEK HEROES HONORED THEIR PROMISE. THEY ASSEMBLED A HUGE FLEET TO FOLLOW HELEN AND PARIS ACROSS THE WINE-DARK SEA. THE SHIPS WERE FILLED WITH WEAPONS AND WARRIORS.
I'D RATHER BE HOME IN ITHACA WITH PENELOPE AND OUR SON. BUT EVEN I COULD NOT FIND A WAY OUT OF OUR PLEDGE.
THERE'S NOTHING LIKE A GOOD WAR FOR BUILDING UP MUSCLES!
YOUR MUSCLES ARE LARGE ENOUGH, MY FRIEND.
WAR IS MORE THAN EXERCISE, AJAX.
IT IS A CHANCE TO GROW IN POWER, RICHES, AND GLORY!
MEANWHILE IN TROY, THE ROYAL FAMILY GREETED PARIS AND HELEN. EVERYONE WAS CHARMED BY HELEN'S BEAUTY—EXCEPT PARIS'S SISTER, CASSANDRA.
WELCOME, MY SON! THESE OLD EYES ARE GLAD TO SEE YOU.
AND DAZZLED BY YOUR COMPANION'S BEAUTY!
WELCOME, PARIS! TO SEE YOU AGAIN BRINGS ME GREAT JOY.
PARIS BRINGS TROY'S DOOM!
IF YOU WILL NOT HEED MY WARNING, AT LEAST RECALL THE PROPHECY MADE AT HIS BIRTH.
DO NOT BE LULLED BY HER BEAUTY. THIS WOMAN WILL BE THE DEATH OF TROY!
PLEASE FORGIVE YOUR SISTER, PARIS. CASSANDRA IS EVER ONE TO SPEAK HER MIND.
TOO BAD SHE'S COMPLETELY MAD! I REALLY MUST MARRY HER OFF TO SOME DISTANT KING.
CASSANDRA! IS THAT ANY WAY TO SPEAK TO YOUR BROTHER AND HIS BELOVED?
THE SUN GOD APOLLO HIMSELF HAD GRANTED CASSANDRA THE GIFT OF PROPHECY. IN EXCHANGE, SHE PROMISED HIM HER LOVE. THEN WH THE GIRL REFUSED THE GOD, APOLL TURNED HER GIFT INTO A CURSE.
O, CRUEL FATE! TO SEE THE TRUTH,
TO SPEAK THE TRUTH, AND NEVER BE BELIEVED!
SO NO ONE HEEDED CASSANDRA'S WARNING. HELEN REMAINED IN TROY. AND IN TIME, HER HUSBAND'S HUGE ARMY ARRIVED.

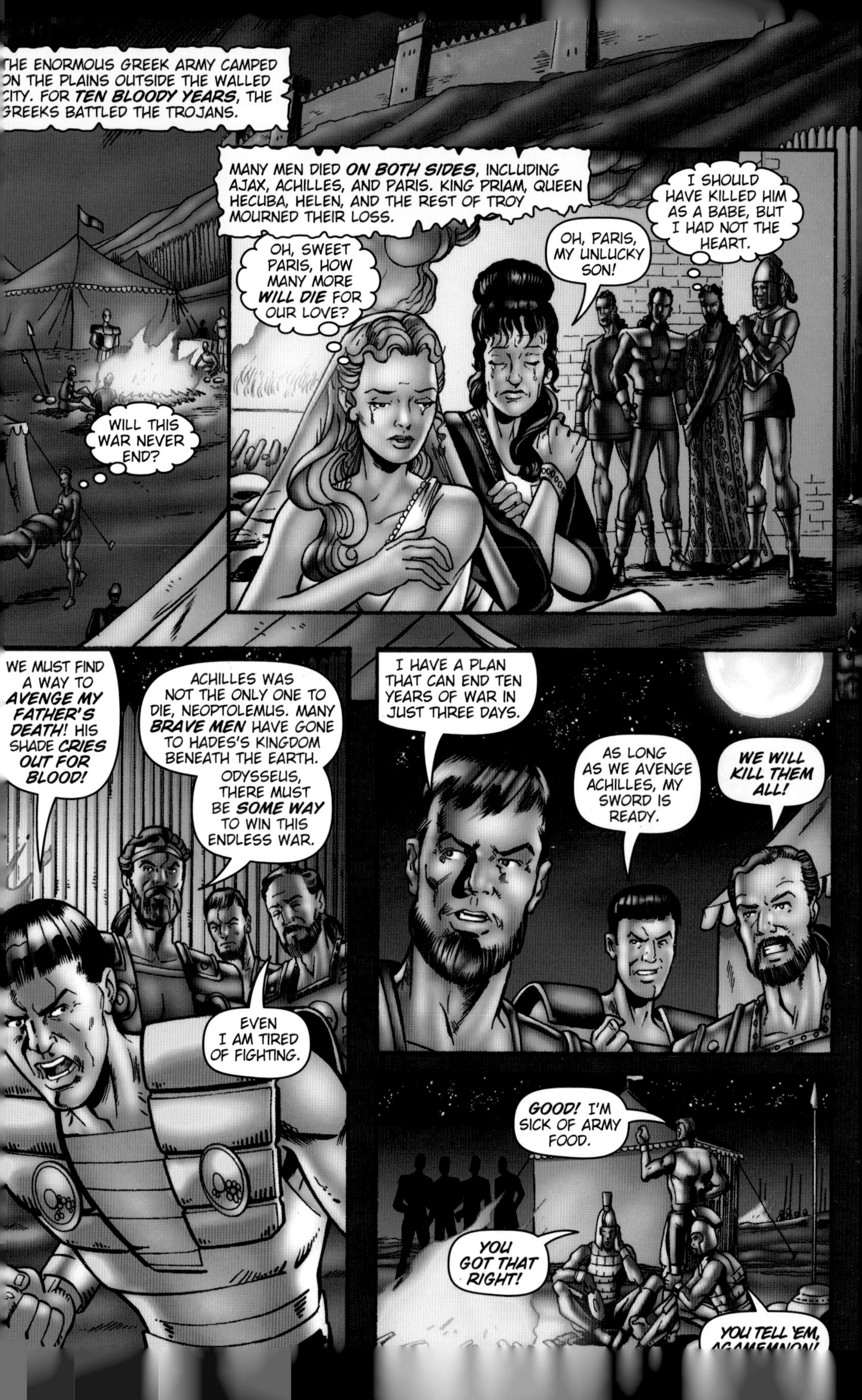
THE ENORMOUS GREEK ARMY CAMPED ON THE PLAINS OUTSIDE THE WALLED CITY. FOR TEN BLOODY YEARS, THE GREEKS BATTLED THE TROJANS.
MANY MEN DIED ON BOTH SIDES, INCLUDING AJAX, ACHILLES, AND PARIS. KING PRIAM, QUEEN HECUBA, HELEN, AND THE REST OF TROY MOURNED THEIR LOSS.
WILL THIS WAR NEVER END?
OH, SWEET PARIS, HOW MANY MORE WILL DIE FOR OUR LOVE?
OH, PARIS, MY UNLUCKY SON!
I SHOULD HAVE KILLED HIM AS A BABE, BUT I HAD NOT THE HEART.
WE MUST FIND A WAY TO AVENGE MY FATHER'S DEATH! HIS SHADE CRIES OUT FOR BLOOD!
ACHILLES WAS NOT THE ONLY ONE TO DIE, NEOPTOLEMUS. MANY BRAVE MEN HAVE GONE TO HADES'S KINGDOM BENEATH THE EARTH.
ODYSSEUS, THERE MUST BE SOME WAY TO WIN THIS ENDLESS WAR.
EVEN I AM TIRED OF FIGHTING.
I HAVE A PLAN THAT CAN END TEN YEARS OF WAR IN JUST THREE DAYS.
AS LONG AS WE AVENGE ACHILLES, MY SWORD IS READY.
WE WILL KILL THEM ALL!
GOOD! I'M SICK OF ARMY FOOD.
YOU GOT THAT RIGHT!
YOU TELL 'EM,

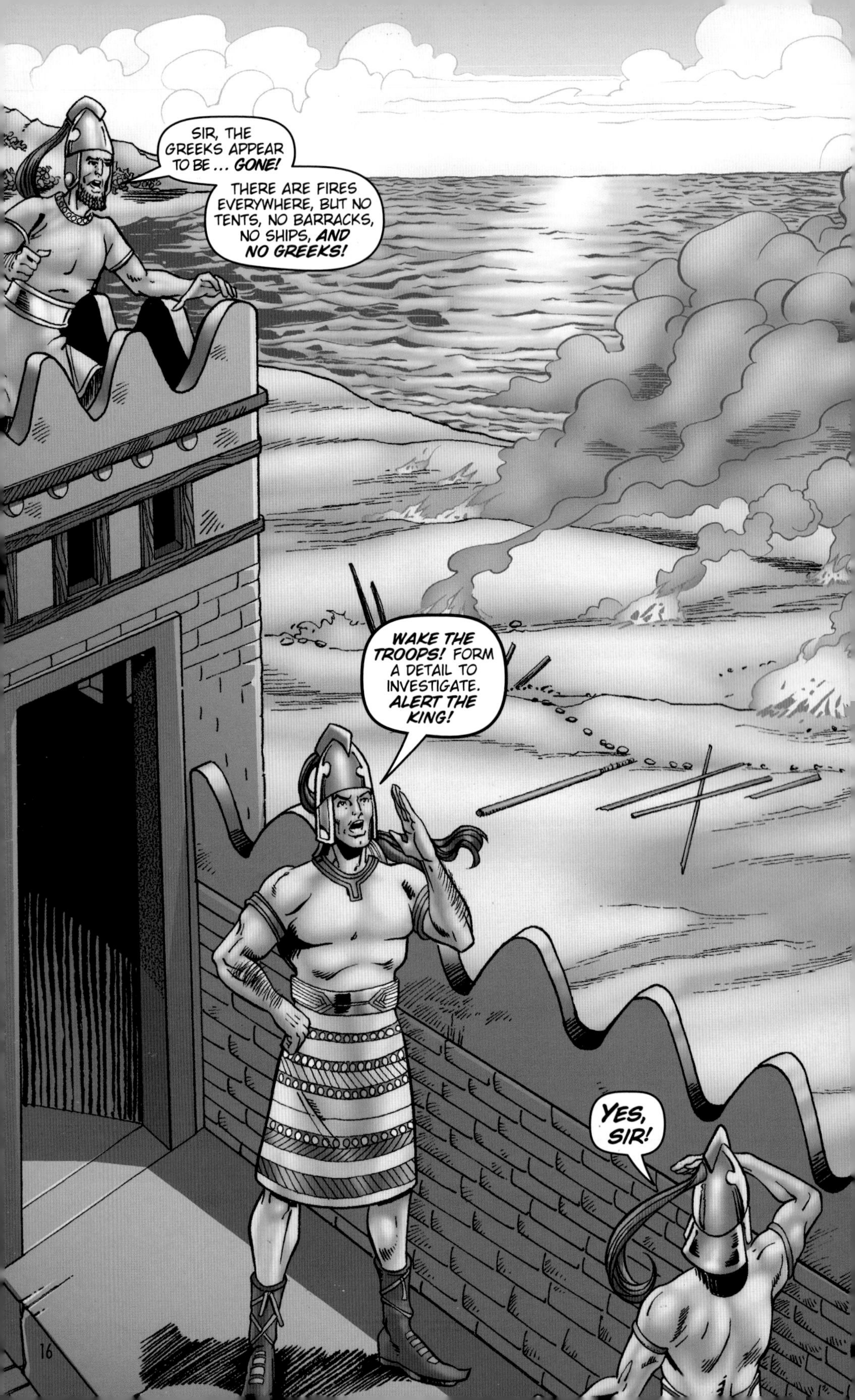
SIR, THE GREEKS APPEAR TO BE ... GONE!
THERE ARE FIRES EVERYWHERE, BUT NO TENTS, NO BARRACKS, NO SHIPS, AND NO GREEKS!
WAKE THE TROOPS! FORM A DETAIL TO INVESTIGATE. ALERT THE KING!
YES, SIR!

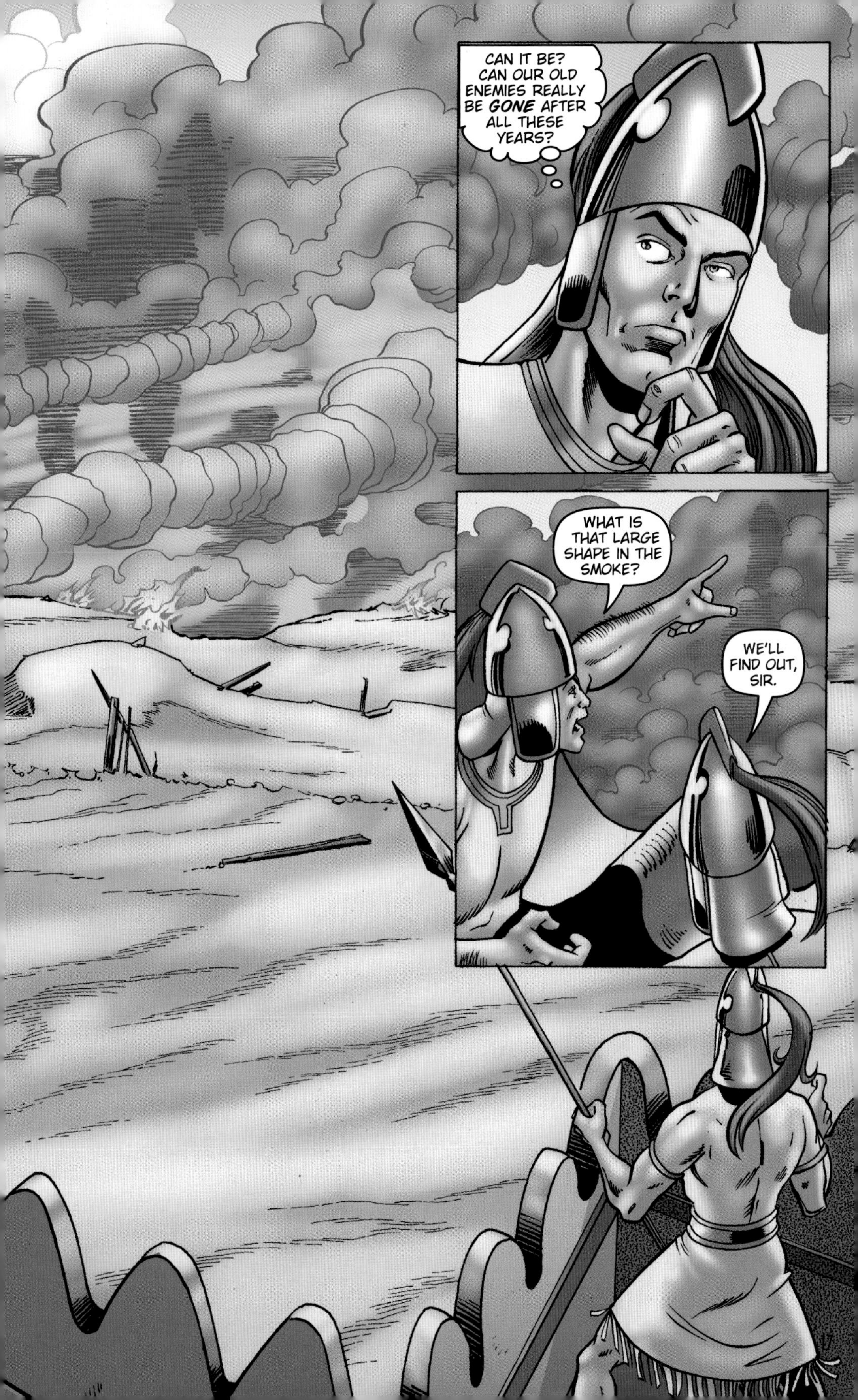
CAN IT BE? CAN OUR OLD ENEMIES REALLY BE **GONE** AFTER ALL THESE YEARS?
WHAT IS THAT LARGE SHAPE IN THE SMOKE?
WE'LL FIND OUT, SIR.

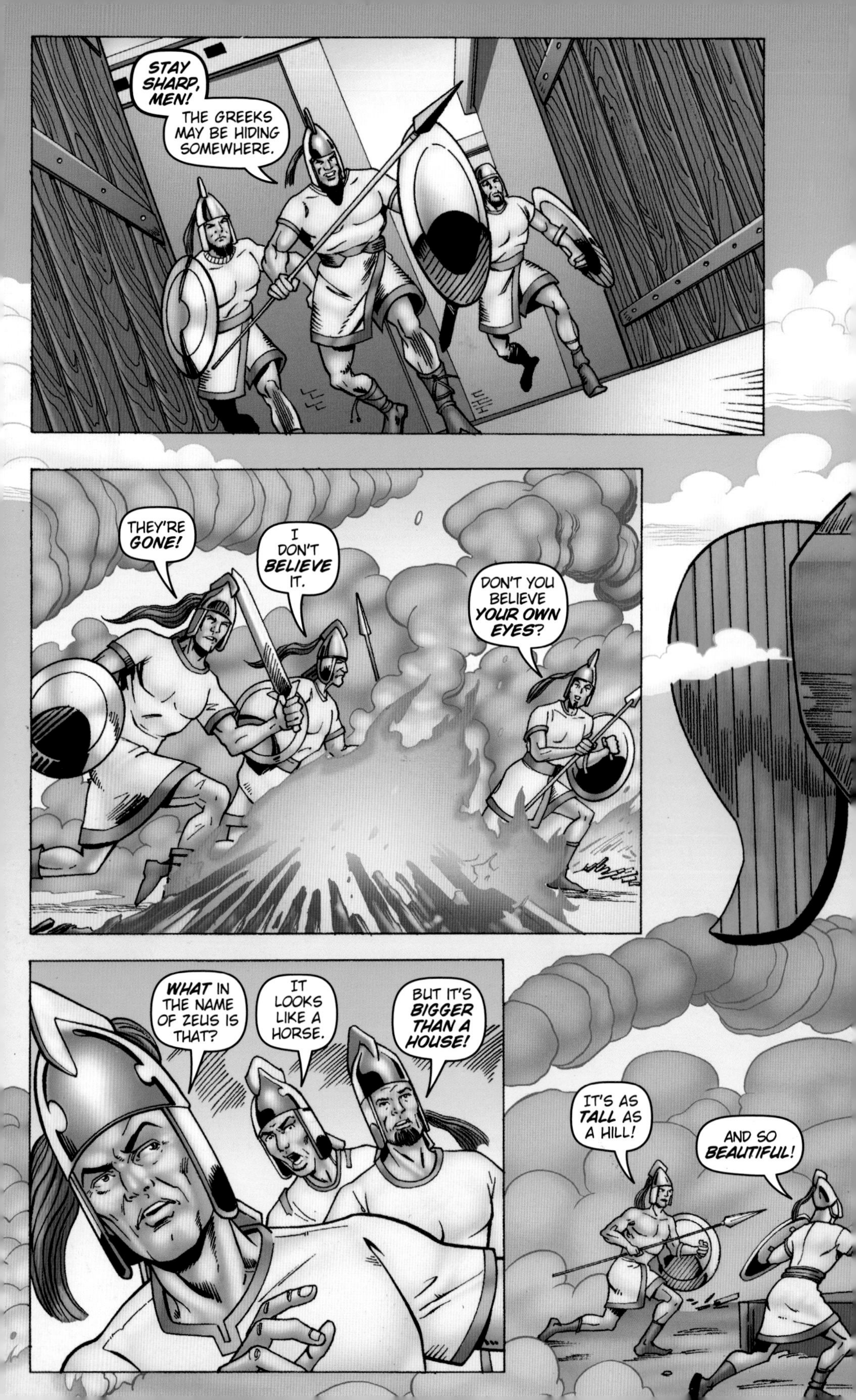
STAY SHARP, MEN!
THE GREEKS MAY BE HIDING SOMEWHERE.
THEY'RE GONE!
I DON'T BELIEVE IT.
DON'T YOU BELIEVE YOUR OWN EYES?
WHAT IN THE NAME OF ZEUS IS THAT?
IT LOOKS LIKE A HORSE.
BUT IT'S BIGGER THAN A HOUSE!
IT'S AS TALL AS A HILL!
AND SO BEAUTIFUL!

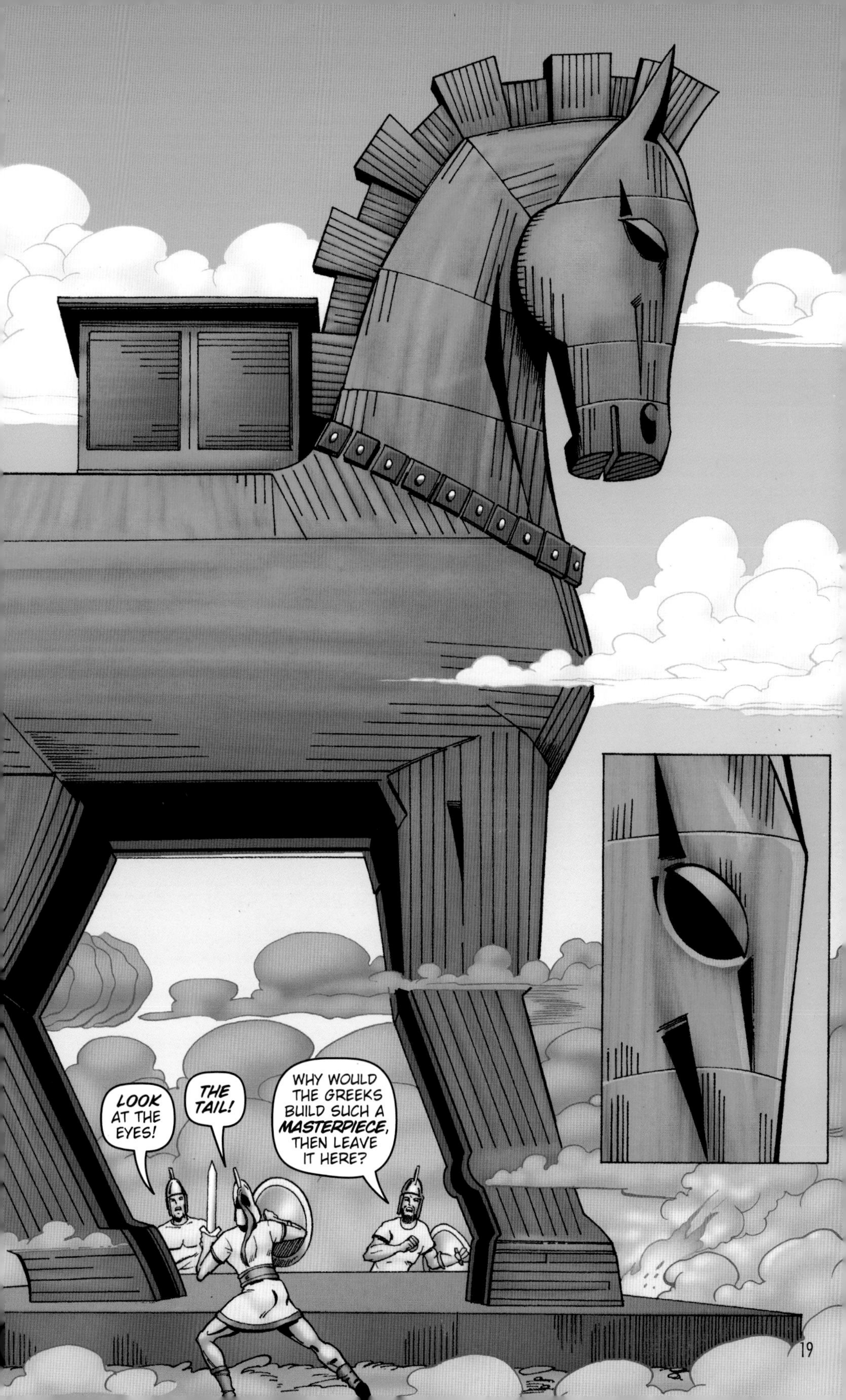
LOOK AT THE EYES!
THE TAIL!
WHY WOULD THE GREEKS BUILD SUCH A MASTERPIECE, THEN LEAVE IT HERE?

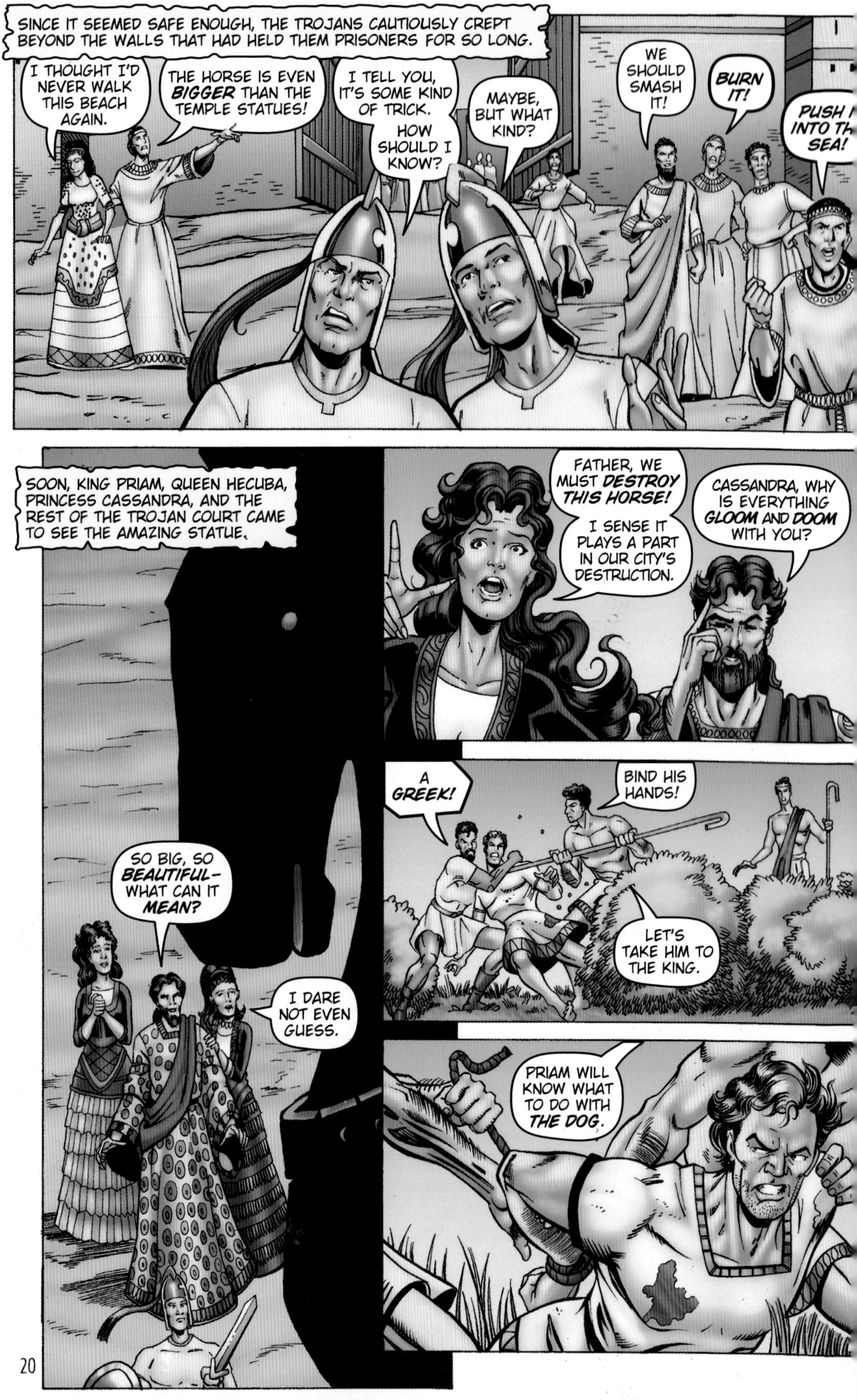
SINCE IT SEEMED SAFE ENOUGH, THE TROJANS CAUTIOUSLY CREPT BEYOND THE WALLS THAT HAD HELD THEM PRISONERS FOR SO LONG.
I THOUGHT I'D NEVER WALK THIS BEACH AGAIN.
THE HORSE IS EVEN BIGGER THAN THE TEMPLE STATUES!
I TELL YOU, IT'S SOME KIND OF TRICK.
HOW SHOULD I KNOW?
MAYBE, BUT WHAT KIND?
WE SHOULD SMASH IT!
BURN IT!
PUSH I INTO TH SEA!
SOON, KING PRIAM, QUEEN HECUBA, PRINCESS CASSANDRA, AND THE REST OF THE TROJAN COURT CAME TO SEE THE AMAZING STATUE.
SO BIG, SO BEAUTIFUL- WHAT CAN IT MEAN?
I DARE NOT EVEN GUESS.
FATHER, WE MUST DESTROY THIS HORSE!
I SENSE IT PLAYS A PART IN OUR CITY'S DESTRUCTION.
CASSANDRA, WHY IS EVERYTHING GLOOM AND DOOM WITH YOU?
A GREEK!
BIND HIS HANDS!
LET'S TAKE HIM TO THE KING.
PRIAM WILL KNOW WHAT TO DO WITH THE DOG.

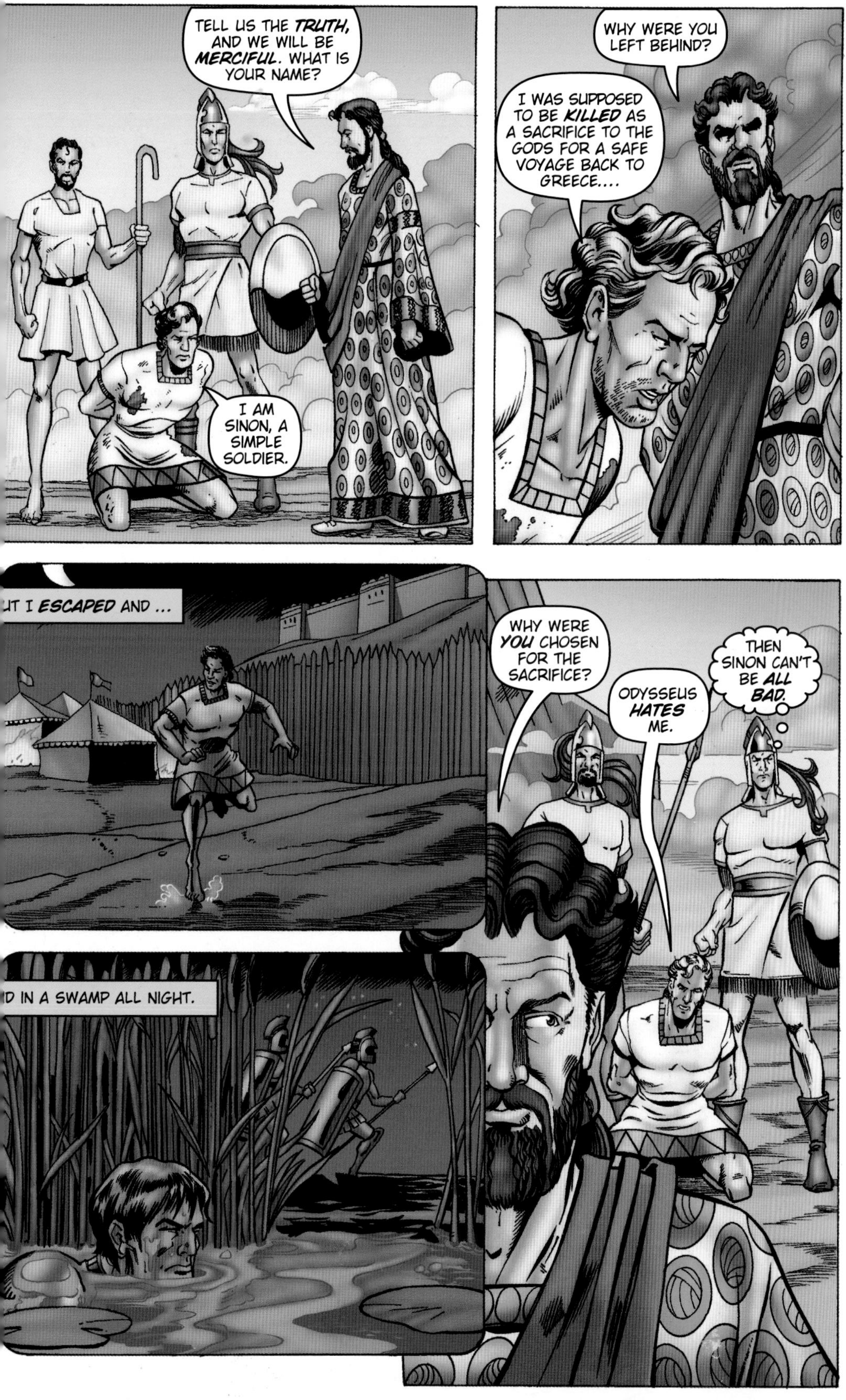
TELL US THE TRUTH, AND WE WILL BE MERCIFUL. WHAT IS YOUR NAME?
I AM SINON, A SIMPLE SOLDIER.
WHY WERE YOU LEFT BEHIND?
I WAS SUPPOSED TO BE KILLED AS A SACRIFICE TO THE GODS FOR A SAFE VOYAGE BACK TO GREECE....
UT I ESCAPED AND ...
D IN A SWAMP ALL NIGHT.
WHY WERE YOU CHOSEN FOR THE SACRIFICE?
ODYSSEUS HATES ME.
THEN SINON CAN'T BE ALL BAD.

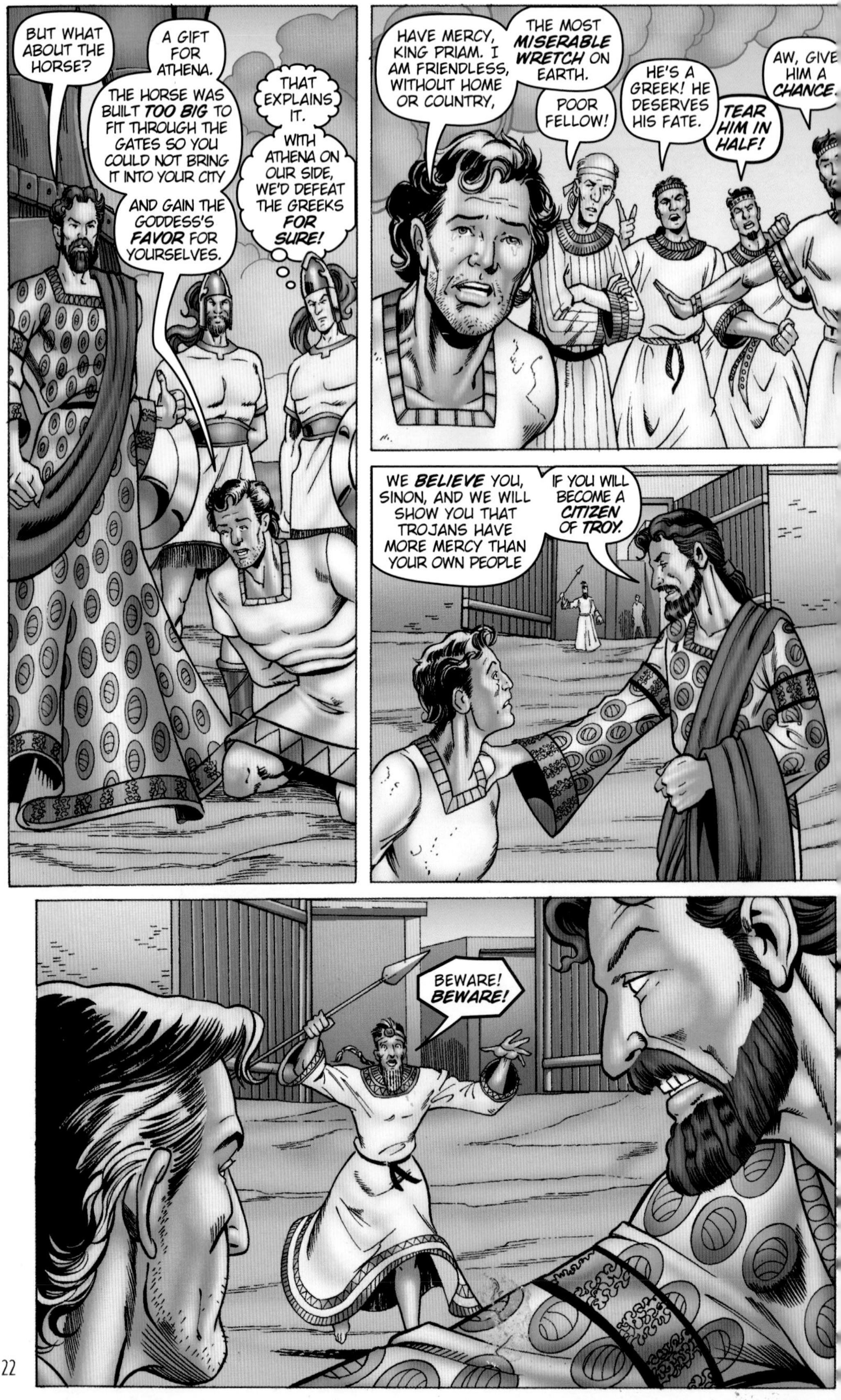

BUT WHAT ABOUT THE HORSE?
A GIFT FOR ATHENA.
THE HORSE WAS BUILT TOO BIG TO FIT THROUGH THE GATES SO YOU COULD NOT BRING IT INTO YOUR CITY
AND GAIN THE GODDESS'S FAVOR FOR YOURSELVES.
THAT EXPLAINS IT.
WITH ATHENA ON OUR SIDE, WE'D DEFEAT THE GREEKS FOR SURE!
HAVE MERCY, KING PRIAM. I AM FRIENDLESS, WITHOUT HOME OR COUNTRY,
THE MOST MISERABLE WRETCH ON EARTH.
POOR FELLOW!
HE'S A GREEK! HE DESERVES HIS FATE.
TEAR HIM IN HALF!
AW, GIVE HIM A CHANCE.
WE BELIEVE YOU, SINON, AND WE WILL SHOW YOU THAT TROJANS HAVE MORE MERCY THAN YOUR OWN PEOPLE
IF YOU WILL BECOME A CITIZEN OF TROY.
BEWARE! BEWARE!

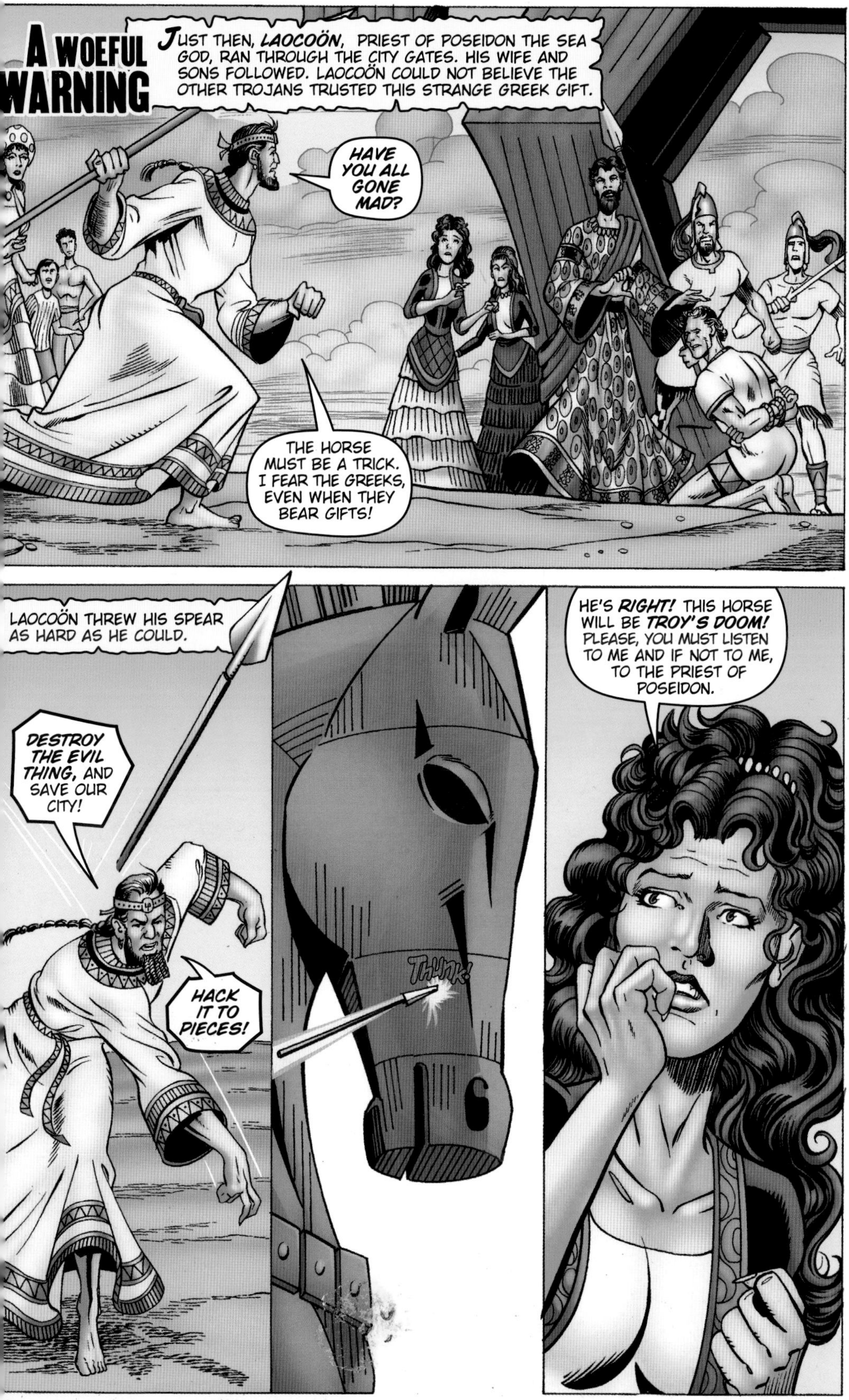
A WOEFUL WARNING
JUST THEN, LAOCOÖN, PRIEST OF POSEIDON THE SEA GOD, RAN THROUGH THE CITY GATES. HIS WIFE AND SONS FOLLOWED. LAOCOÖN COULD NOT BELIEVE THE OTHER TROJANS TRUSTED THIS STRANGE GREEK GIFT.
HAVE YOU ALL GONE MAD?
THE HORSE MUST BE A TRICK. I FEAR THE GREEKS, EVEN WHEN THEY BEAR GIFTS!
LAOCOÖN THREW HIS SPEAR AS HARD AS HE COULD.
DESTROY THE EVIL THING, AND SAVE OUR CITY!
HACK IT TO PIECES!
THUNK!
HE'S RIGHT! THIS HORSE WILL BE TROY'S DOOM! PLEASE, YOU MUST LISTEN TO ME AND IF NOT TO ME, TO THE PRIEST OF POSEIDON.

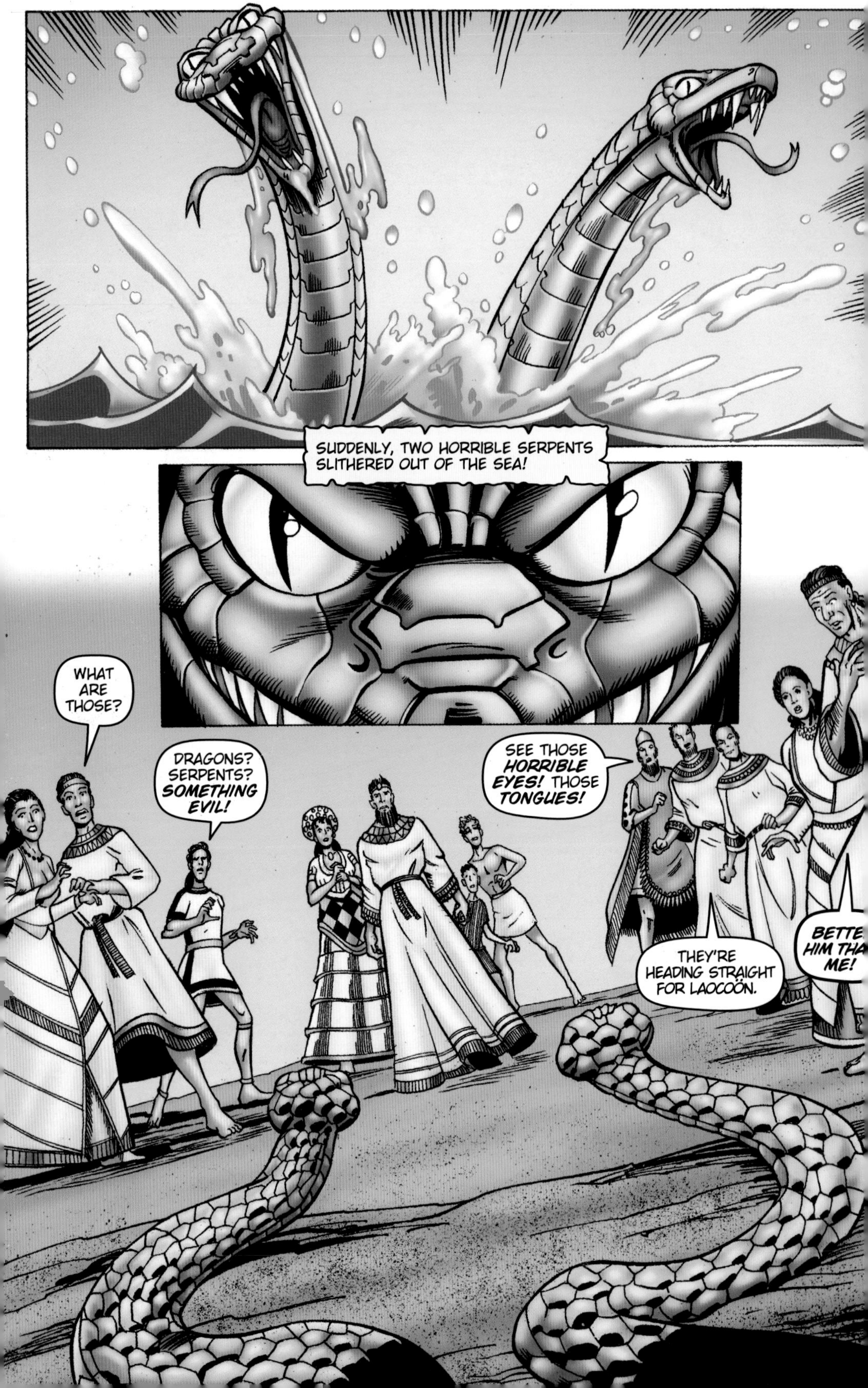
SUDDENLY, TWO HORRIBLE SERPENTS SLITHERED OUT OF THE SEA!
WHAT ARE THOSE?
DRAGONS? SERPENTS? SOMETHING EVIL!
SEE THOSE HORRIBLE EYES! THOSE TONGUES!
THEY'RE HEADING STRAIGHT FOR LAOCOÖN.

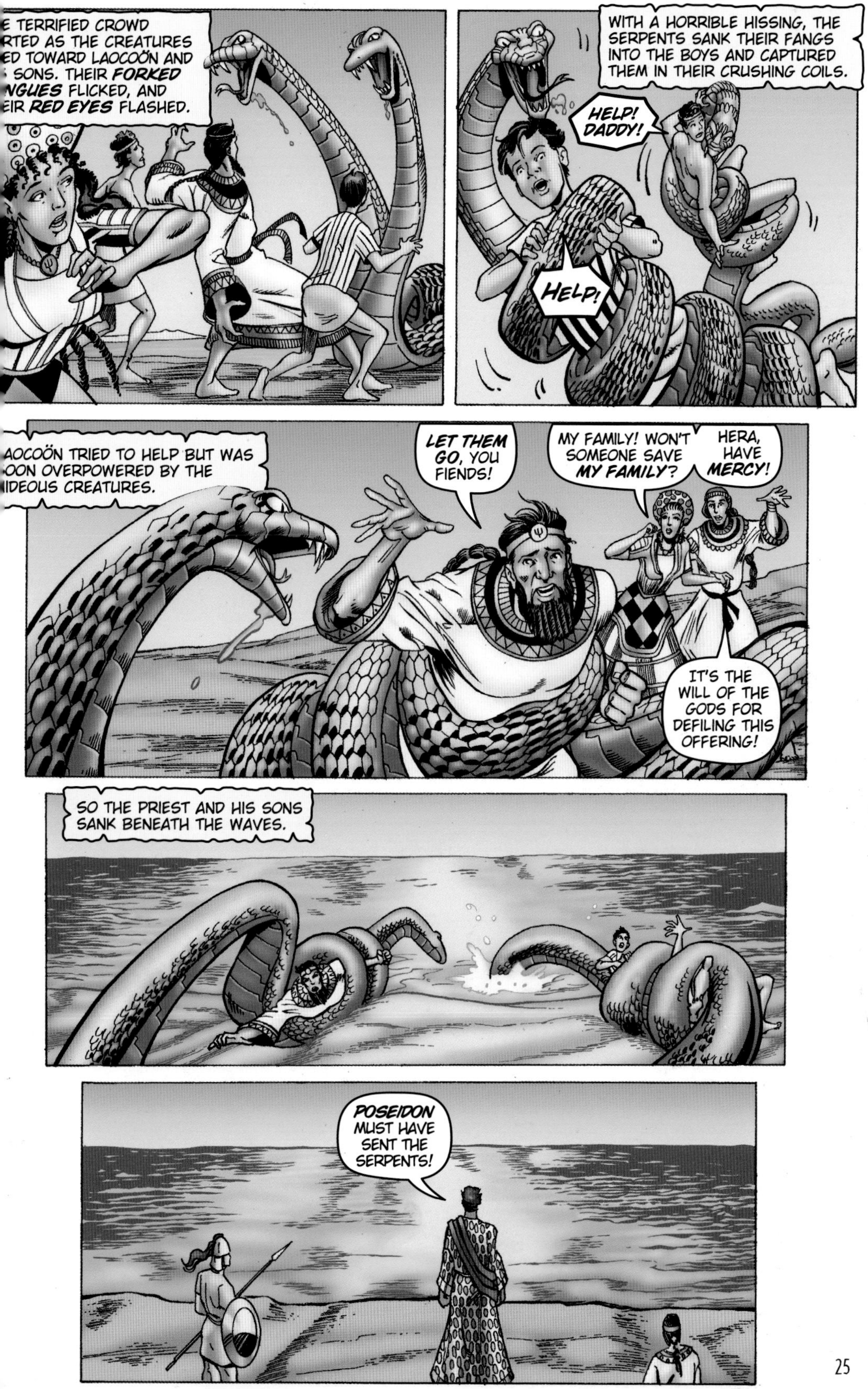

E TERRIFIED CROWD
RTED AS THE CREATURES
ED TOWARD LAOCOÖN AND
SONS. THEIR FORKED
NGUES FLICKED, AND
EIR RED EYES FLASHED.
WITH A HORRIBLE HISSING, THE SERPENTS SANK THEIR FANGS INTO THE BOYS AND CAPTURED THEM IN THEIR CRUSHING COILS.
HELP! DADDY!
HELP!
AOCOÖN TRIED TO HELP BUT WAS
OON OVERPOWERED BY THE
IDEOUS CREATURES.
LET THEM GO, YOU FIENDS!
MY FAMILY! WON'T SOMEONE SAVE MY FAMILY?
HERA, HAVE MERCY!
IT'S THE WILL OF THE GODS FOR DEFILING THIS OFFERING!
SO THE PRIEST AND HIS SONS SANK BENEATH THE WAVES.
POSEIDON MUST HAVE SENT THE SERPENTS!

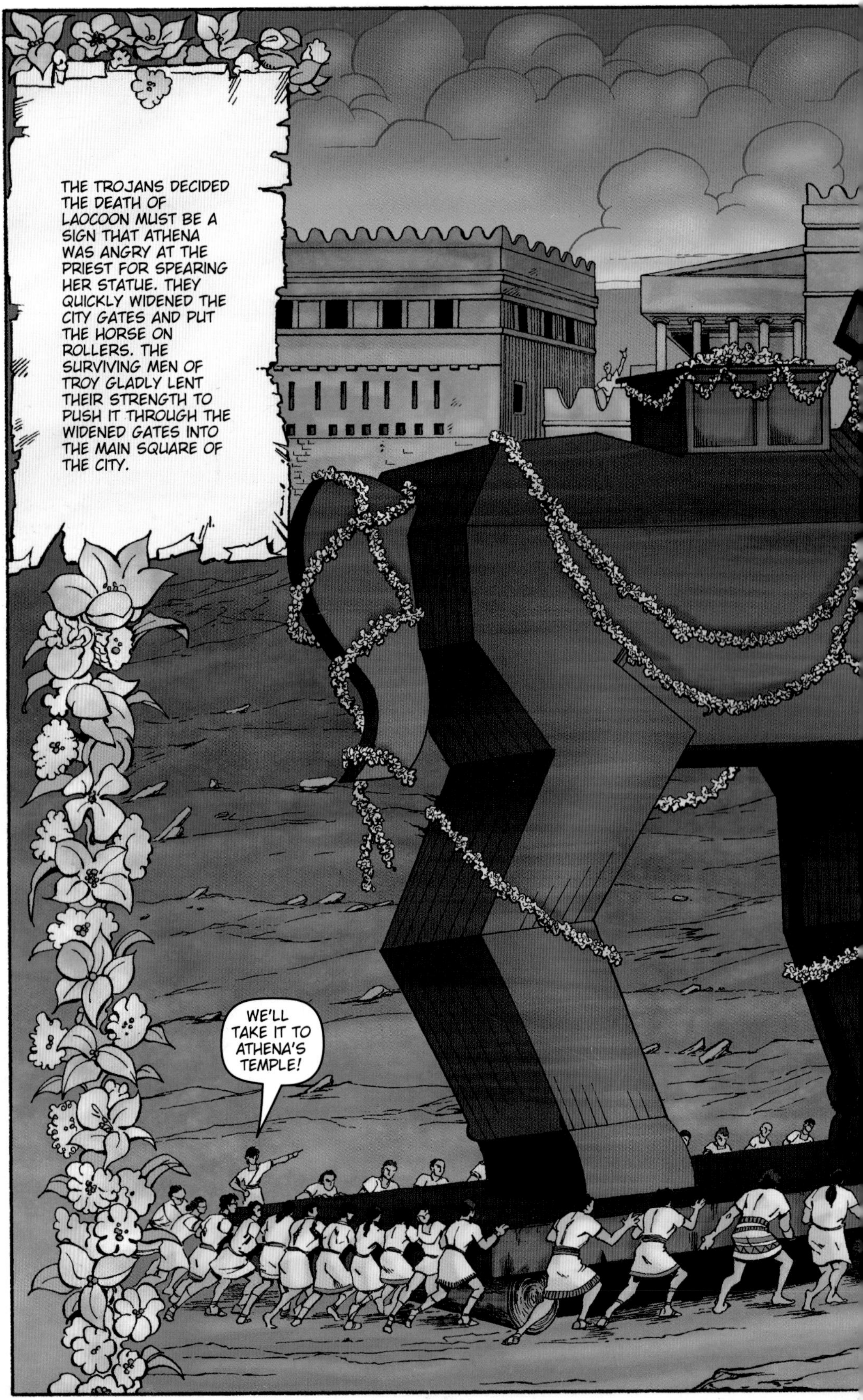
THE TROJANS DECIDED THE DEATH OF LAOCOON MUST BE A SIGN THAT ATHENA WAS ANGRY AT THE PRIEST FOR SPEARING HER STATUE. THEY QUICKLY WIDENED THE CITY GATES AND PUT THE HORSE ON ROLLERS. THE SURVIVING MEN OF TROY GLADLY LENT THEIR STRENGTH TO PUSH IT THROUGH THE WIDENED GATES INTO THE MAIN SQUARE OF THE CITY.
WE'LL TAKE IT TO ATHENA'S TEMPLE!

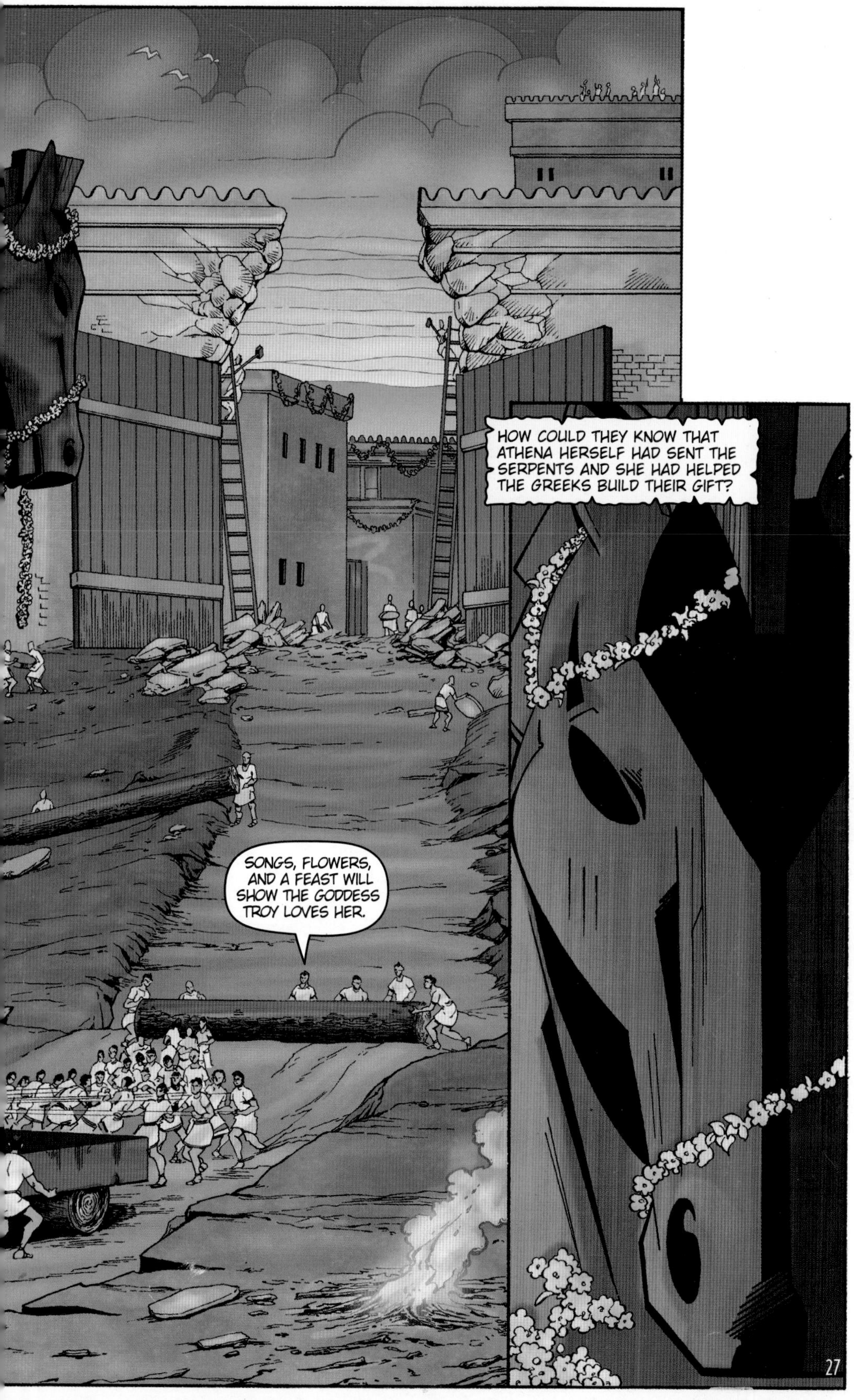
SONGS, FLOWERS, AND A FEAST WILL SHOW THE GODDESS TROY LOVES HER.
HOW COULD THEY KNOW THAT ATHENA HERSELF HAD SENT THE SERPENTS AND SHE HAD HELPED THE GREEKS BUILD THEIR GIFT?

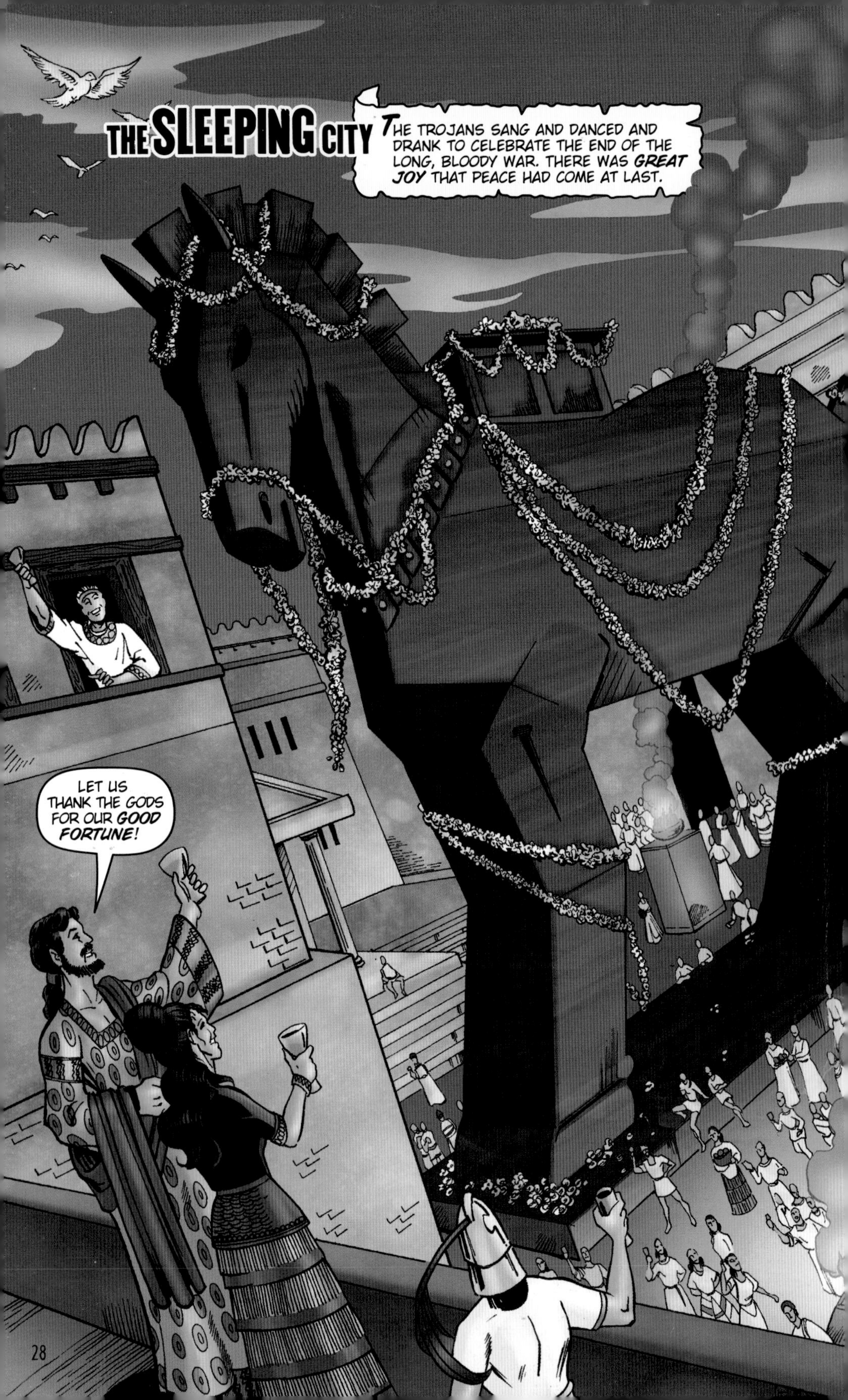
THE SLEEPING CITY
THE TROJANS SANG AND DANCED AND DRANK TO CELEBRATE THE END OF THE LONG, BLOODY WAR. THERE WAS GREAT JOY THAT PEACE HAD COME AT LAST.
LET US THANK THE GODS FOR OUR GOOD FORTUNE!

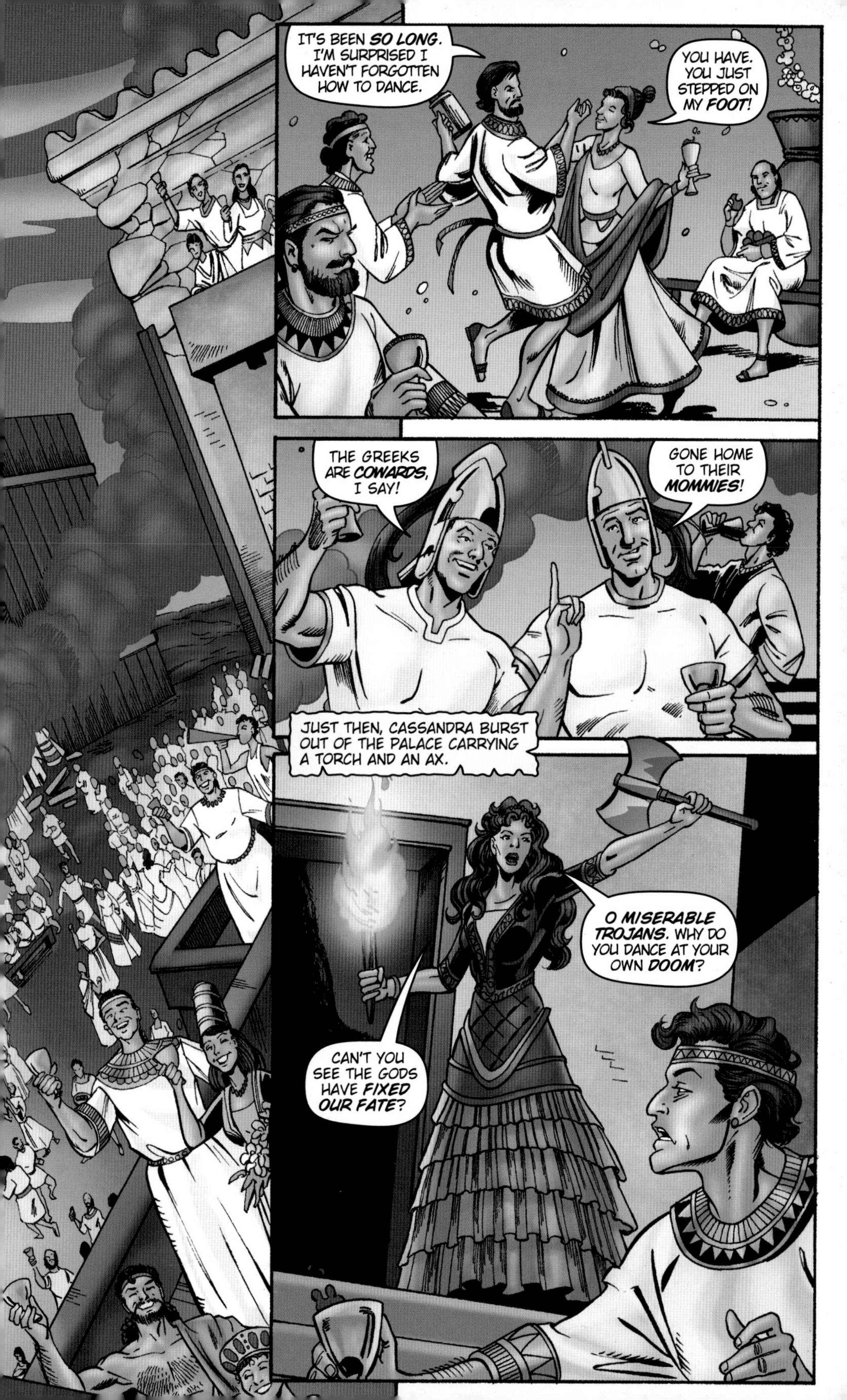

IT'S BEEN **SO LONG**. I'M SURPRISED I HAVEN'T FORGOTTEN HOW TO DANCE.
YOU HAVE. YOU JUST STEPPED ON MY **FOOT**!
THE GREEKS ARE **COWARDS**, I SAY!
GONE HOME TO THEIR **MOMMIES**!
JUST THEN, CASSANDRA BURST OUT OF THE PALACE CARRYING A TORCH AND AN AX.
O MISERABLE TROJANS. WHY DO YOU DANCE AT YOUR OWN **DOOM**?
CAN'T YOU SEE THE GODS HAVE **FIXED OUR FATE**?

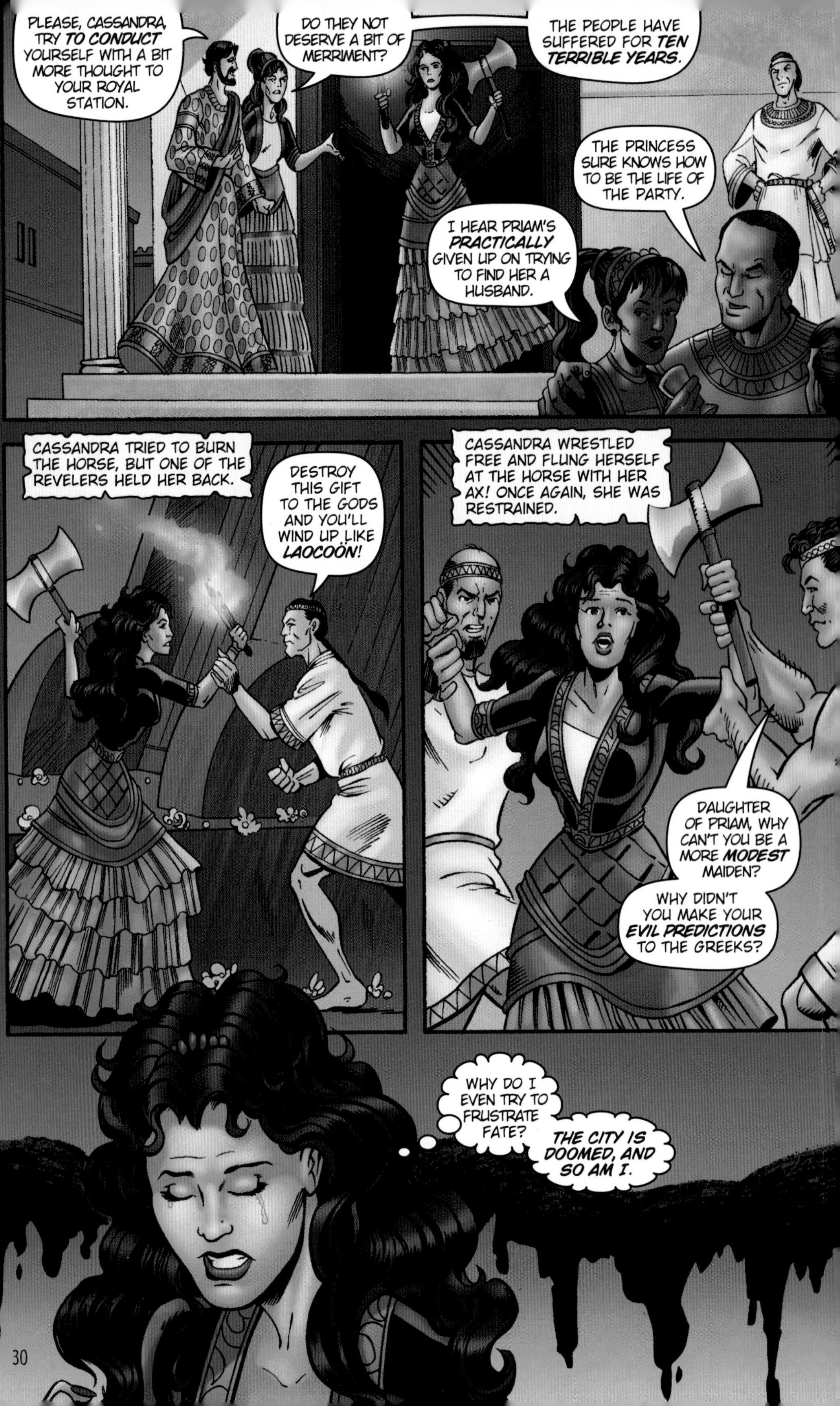
PLEASE, CASSANDRA, TRY TO CONDUCT YOURSELF WITH A BIT MORE THOUGHT TO YOUR ROYAL STATION.
DO THEY NOT DESERVE A BIT OF MERRIMENT?
THE PEOPLE HAVE SUFFERED FOR TEN TERRIBLE YEARS.
THE PRINCESS SURE KNOWS HOW TO BE THE LIFE OF THE PARTY.
I HEAR PRIAM'S PRACTICALLY GIVEN UP ON TRYING TO FIND HER A HUSBAND.
CASSANDRA TRIED TO BURN THE HORSE, BUT ONE OF THE REVELERS HELD HER BACK.
DESTROY THIS GIFT TO THE GODS AND YOU'LL WIND UP LIKE LAOCOÖN!
CASSANDRA WRESTLED FREE AND FLUNG HERSELF AT THE HORSE WITH HER AX! ONCE AGAIN, SHE WAS RESTRAINED.
DAUGHTER OF PRIAM, WHY CAN'T YOU BE A MORE MODEST MAIDEN?
WHY DIDN'T YOU MAKE YOUR EVIL PREDICTIONS TO THE GREEKS?
WHY DO I EVEN TRY TO FRUSTRATE FATE?
THE CITY IS DOOMED, AND SO AM I.

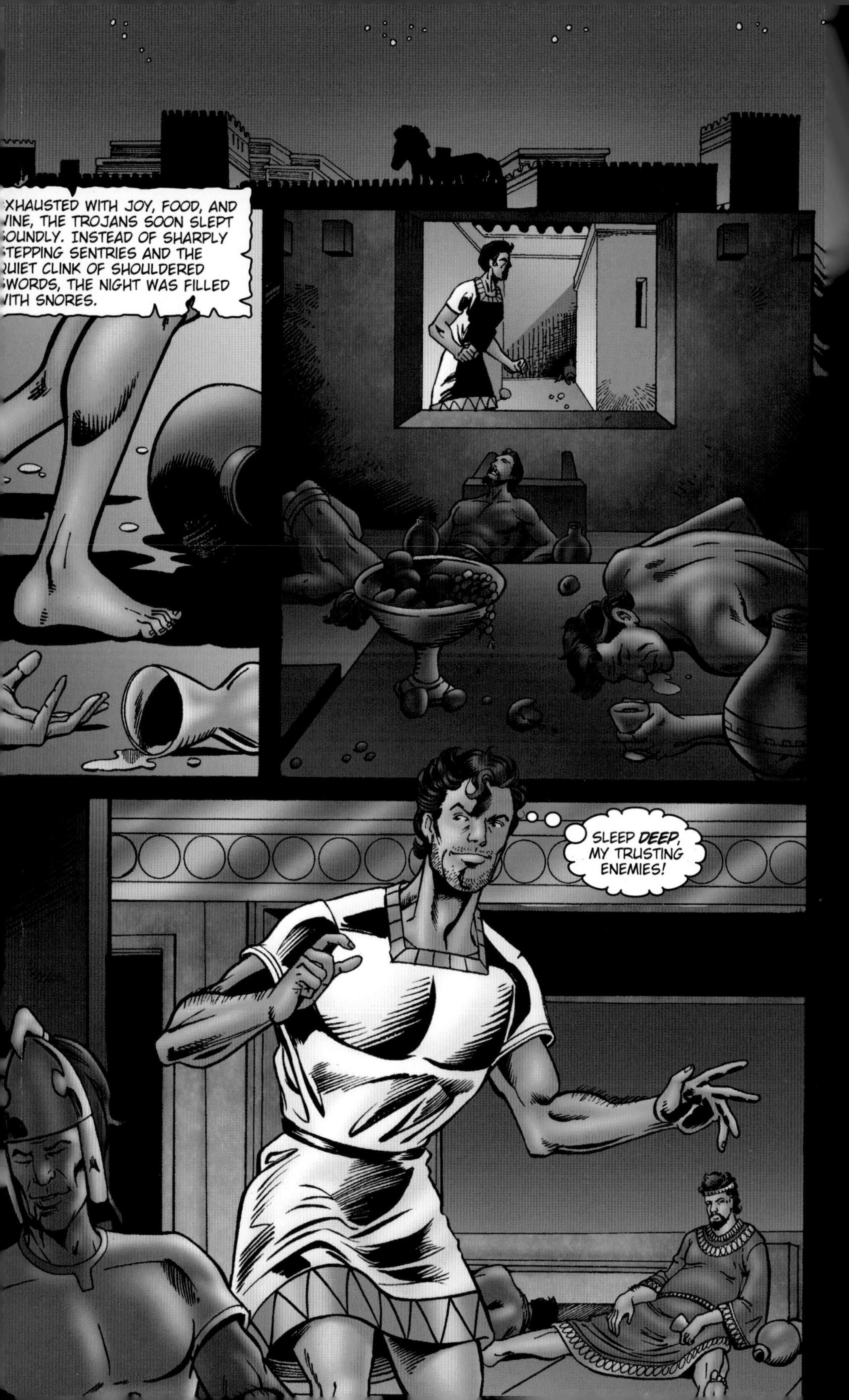
XHAUSTED WITH JOY, FOOD, AND INE, THE TROJANS SOON SLEPT OUNDLY. INSTEAD OF SHARPLY TEPPING SENTRIES AND THE UIET CLINK OF SHOULDERED WORDS, THE NIGHT WAS FILLED ITH SNORES.
SLEEP DEEP, MY TRUSTING ENEMIES!

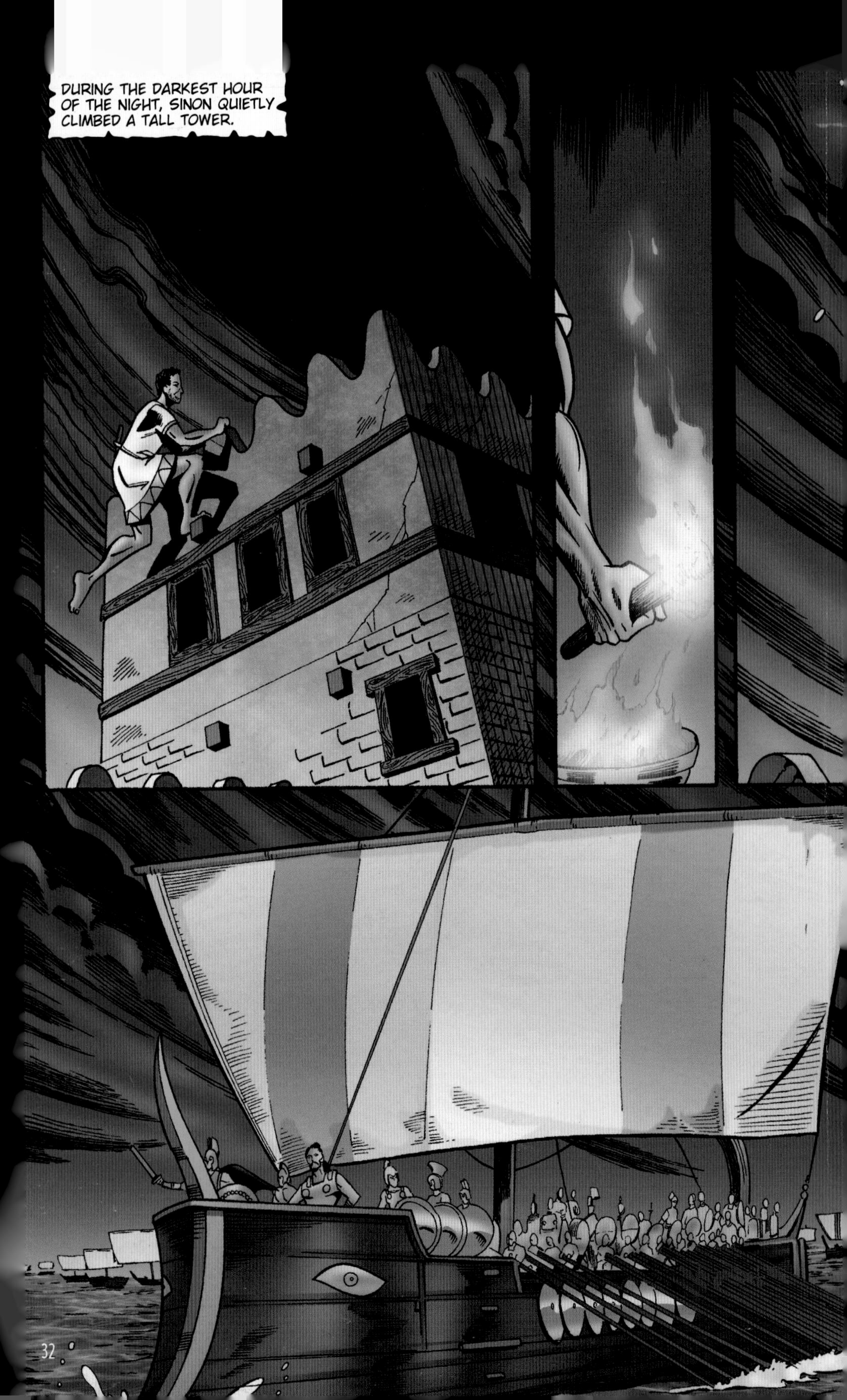
DURING THE DARKEST HOUR OF THE NIGHT, SINON QUIETLY CLIMBED A TALL TOWER.

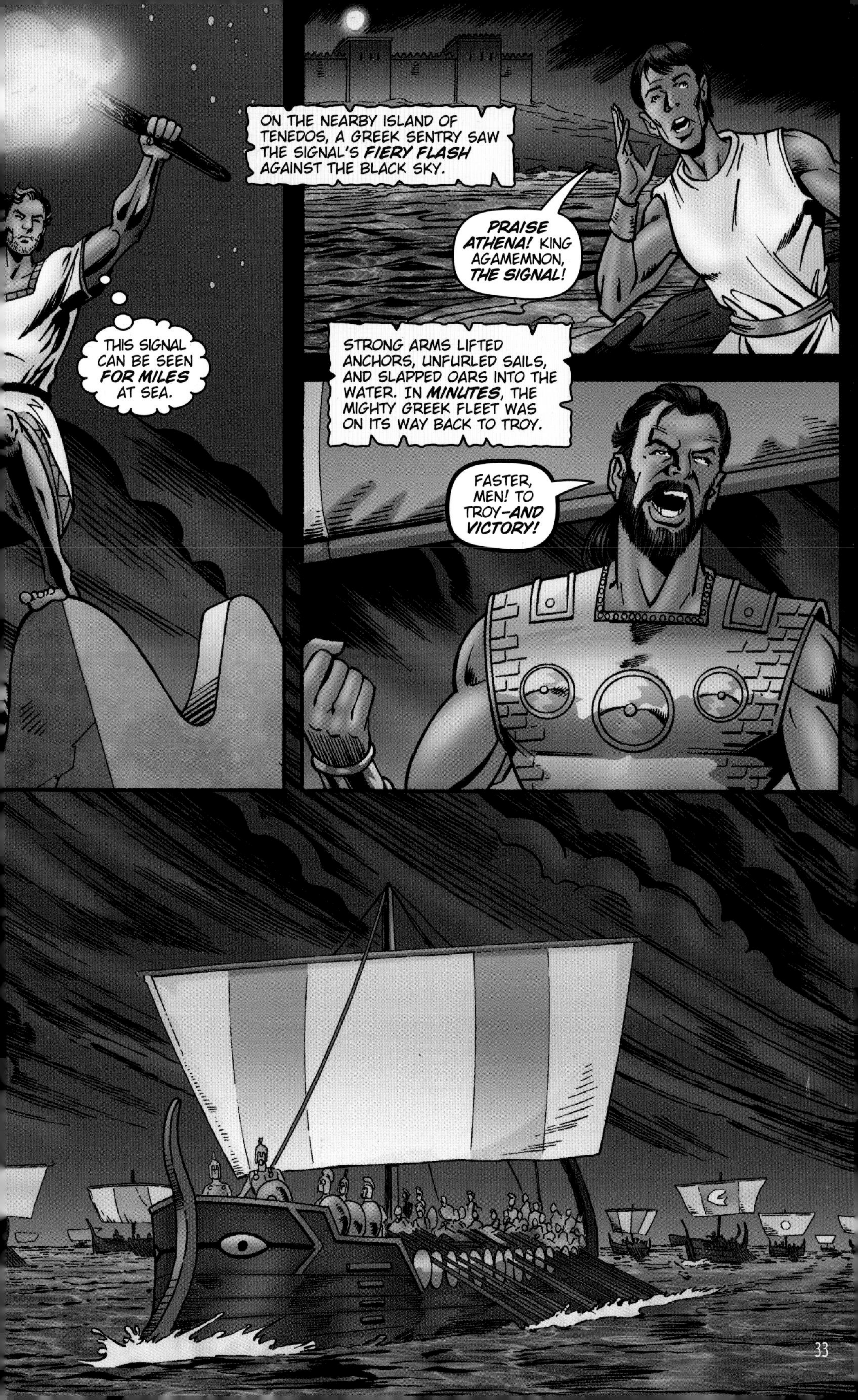
THIS SIGNAL CAN BE SEEN FOR MILES AT SEA.
ON THE NEARBY ISLAND OF TENEDOS, A GREEK SENTRY SAW THE SIGNAL'S FIERY FLASH AGAINST THE BLACK SKY.
PRAISE ATHENA! KING AGAMEMNON, THE SIGNAL!
STRONG ARMS LIFTED ANCHORS, UNFURLED SAILS, AND SLAPPED OARS INTO THE WATER. IN MINUTES, THE MIGHTY GREEK FLEET WAS ON ITS WAY BACK TO TROY.
FASTER, MEN! TO TROY—AND VICTORY!

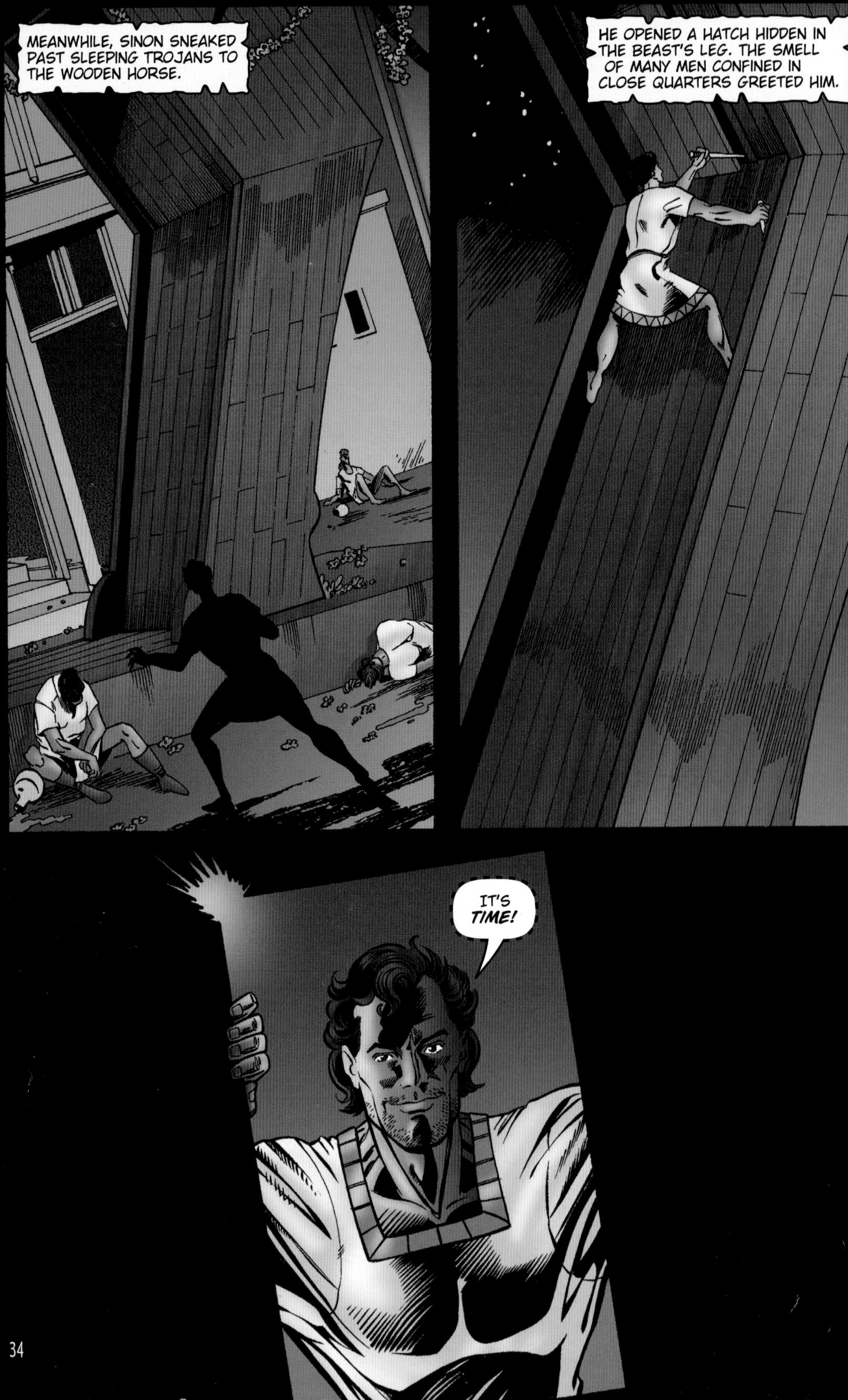
MEANWHILE, SINON SNEAKED PAST SLEEPING TROJANS TO THE WOODEN HORSE.
HE OPENED A HATCH HIDDEN IN THE BEAST'S LEG. THE SMELL OF MANY MEN CONFINED IN CLOSE QUARTERS GREETED HIM.
IT'S *TIME!*

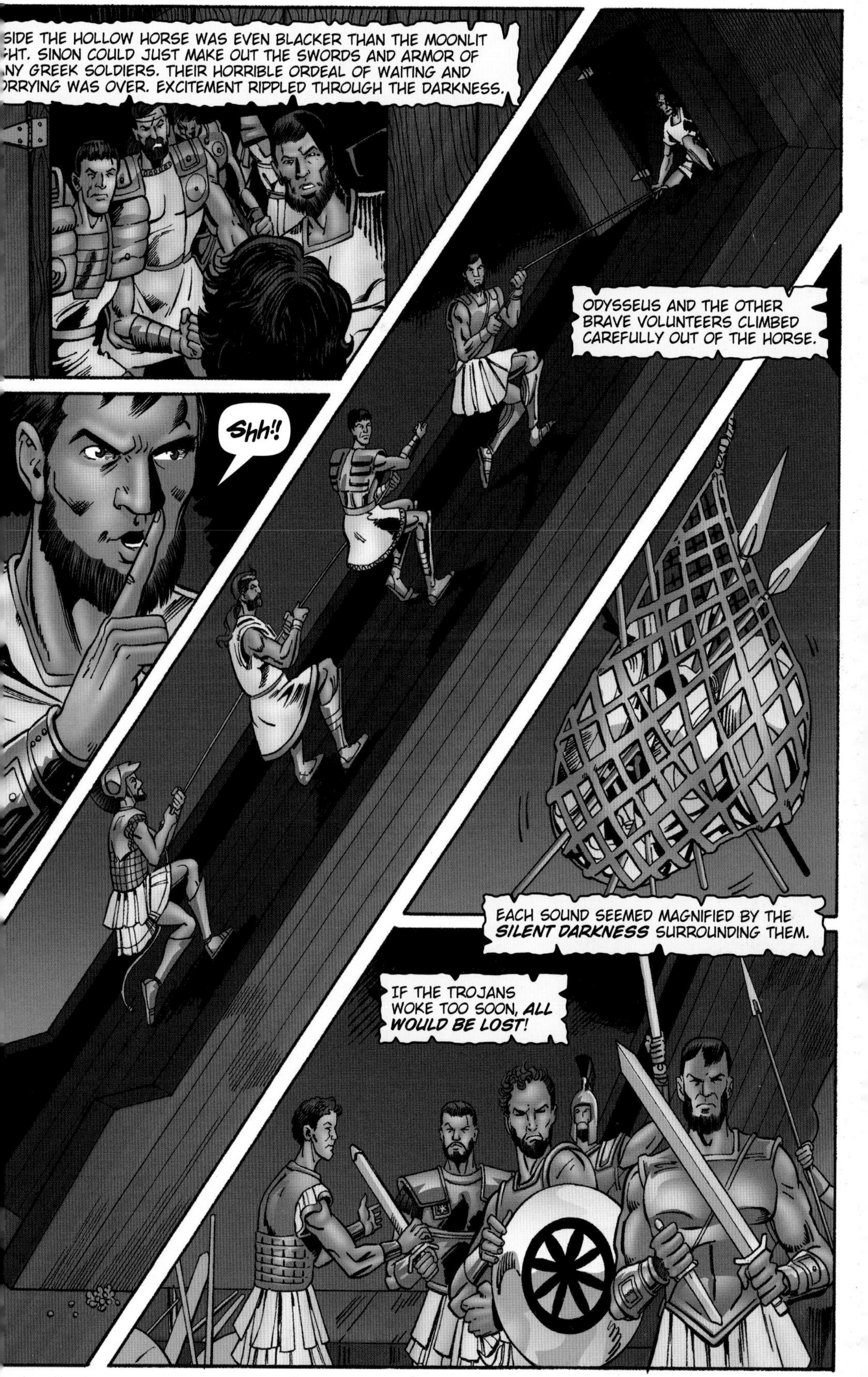

SIDE THE HOLLOW HORSE WAS EVEN BLACKER THAN THE MOONLIT
GHT. SINON COULD JUST MAKE OUT THE SWORDS AND ARMOR OF
NY GREEK SOLDIERS. THEIR HORRIBLE ORDEAL OF WAITING AND
ORRYING WAS OVER. EXCITEMENT RIPPLED THROUGH THE DARKNESS.
Shh!!
ODYSSEUS AND THE OTHER BRAVE VOLUNTEERS CLIMBED CAREFULLY OUT OF THE HORSE.
EACH SOUND SEEMED MAGNIFIED BY THE SILENT DARKNESS SURROUNDING THEM.
IF THE TROJANS WOKE TOO SOON, ALL WOULD BE LOST!

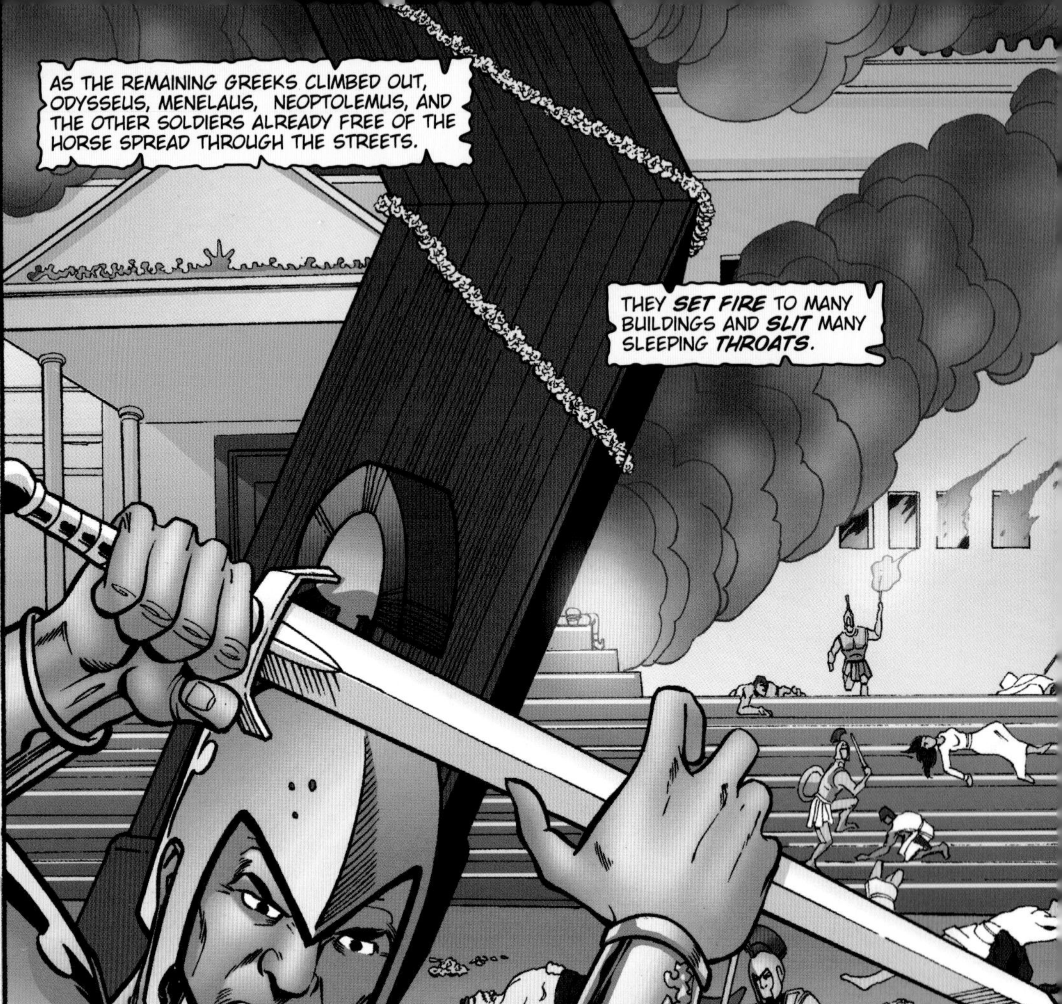
AS THE REMAINING GREEKS CLIMBED OUT, ODYSSEUS, MENELAUS, NEOPTOLEMUS, AND THE OTHER SOLDIERS ALREADY FREE OF THE HORSE SPREAD THROUGH THE STREETS.
THEY SET FIRE TO MANY BUILDINGS AND SLIT MANY SLEEPING THROATS.

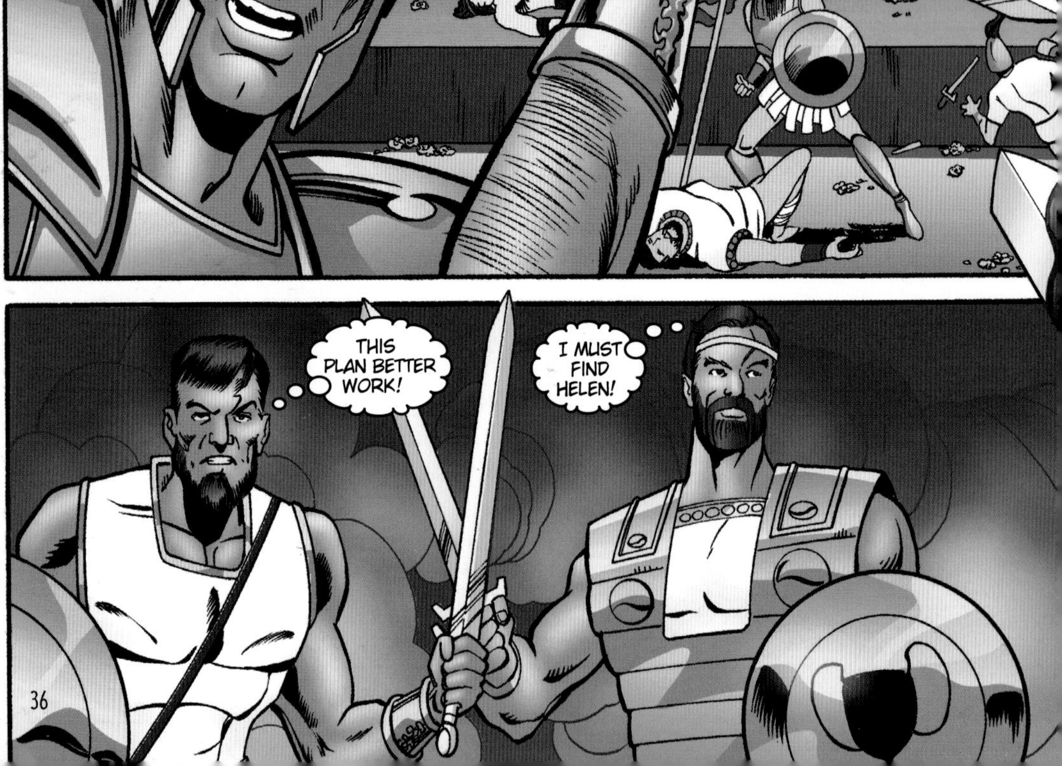
THIS PLAN BETTER WORK!
I MUST FIND HELEN!

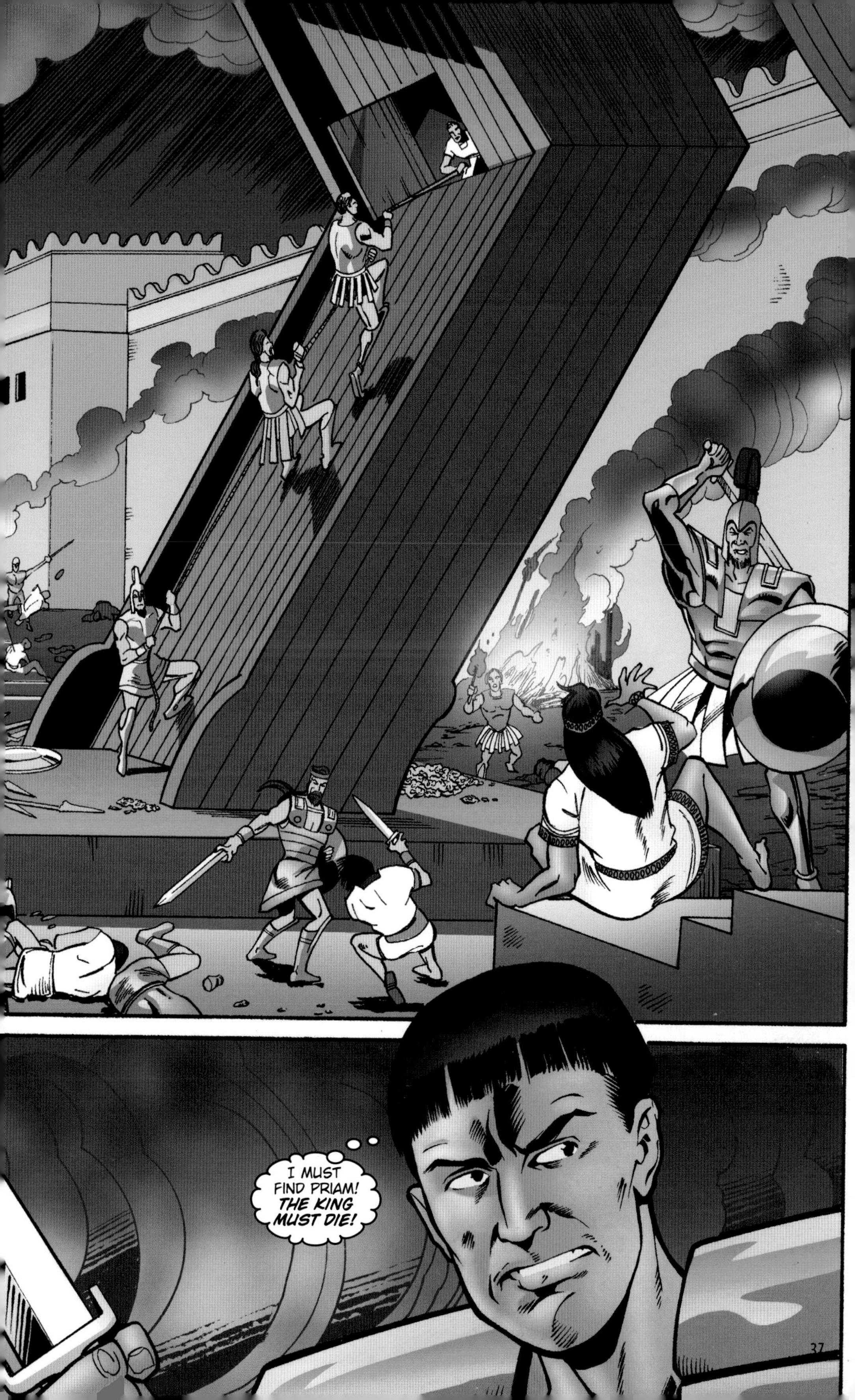
I MUST FIND PRIAM! THE KING MUST DIE!

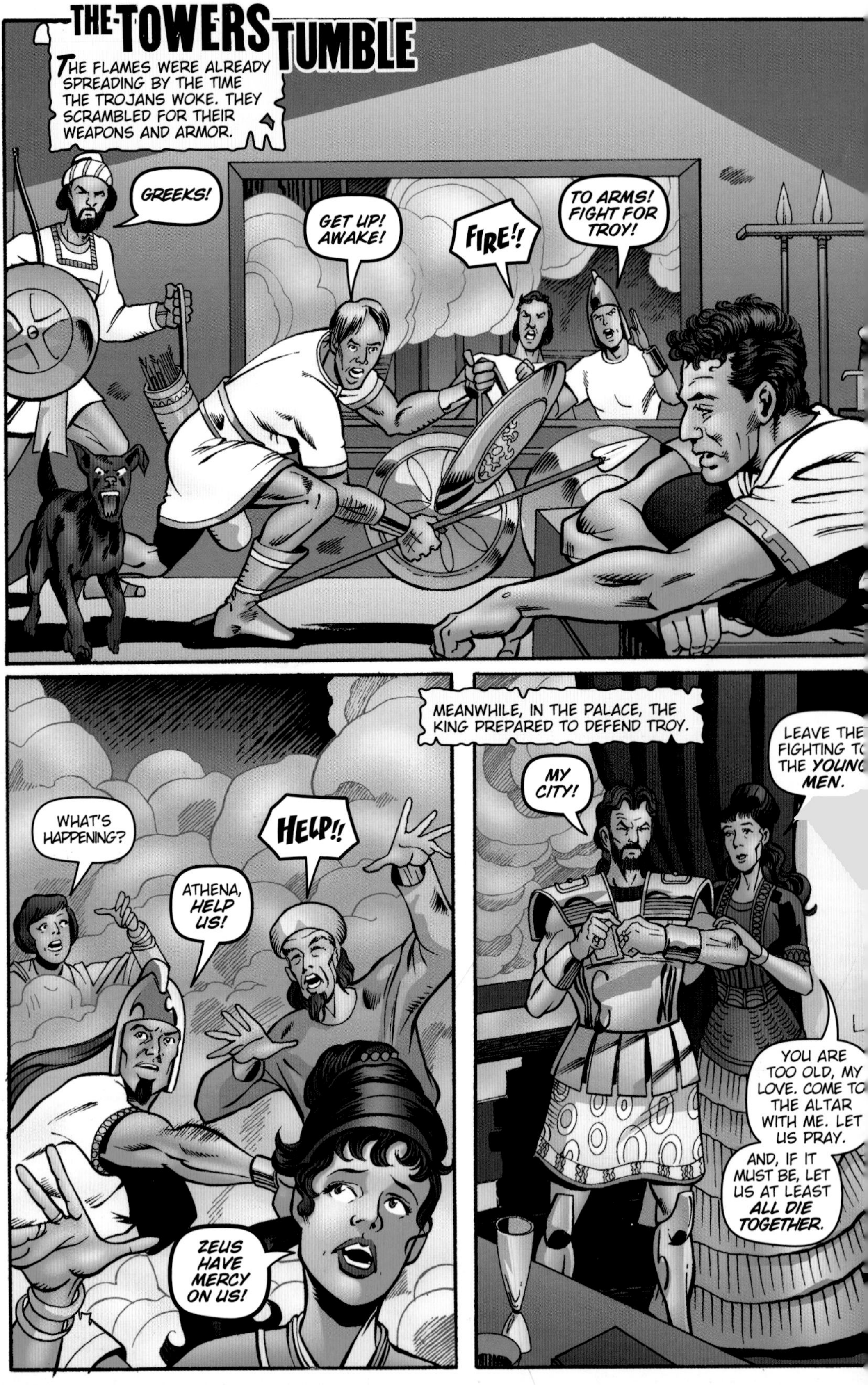
THE TOWERS TUMBLE
THE FLAMES WERE ALREADY SPREADING BY THE TIME THE TROJANS WOKE. THEY SCRAMBLED FOR THEIR WEAPONS AND ARMOR.
GREEKS!
GET UP! AWAKE!
FIRE!!
TO ARMS! FIGHT FOR TROY!
WHAT'S HAPPENING?
HELP!!
ATHENA, HELP US!
ZEUS HAVE MERCY ON US!
MEANWHILE, IN THE PALACE, THE KING PREPARED TO DEFEND TROY.
MY CITY!
LEAVE THE FIGHTING TO THE YOUNG MEN.
YOU ARE TOO OLD, MY LOVE. COME TO THE ALTAR WITH ME. LET US PRAY.
AND, IF IT MUST BE, LET US AT LEAST ALL DIE TOGETHER.

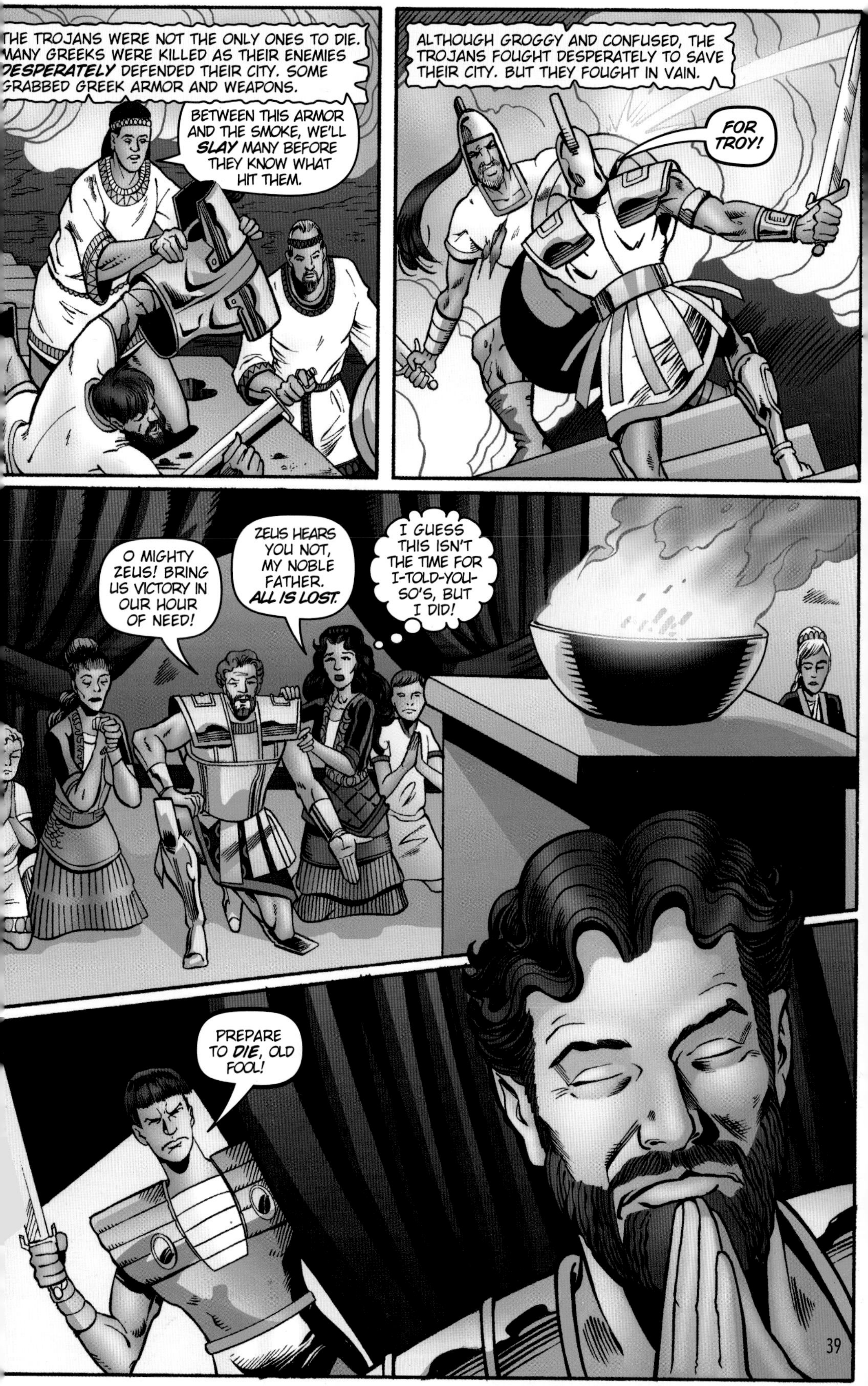
THE TROJANS WERE NOT THE ONLY ONES TO DIE. MANY GREEKS WERE KILLED AS THEIR ENEMIES DESPERATELY DEFENDED THEIR CITY. SOME GRABBED GREEK ARMOR AND WEAPONS.
BETWEEN THIS ARMOR AND THE SMOKE, WE'LL SLAY MANY BEFORE THEY KNOW WHAT HIT THEM.
ALTHOUGH GROGGY AND CONFUSED, THE TROJANS FOUGHT DESPERATELY TO SAVE THEIR CITY. BUT THEY FOUGHT IN VAIN.
FOR TROY!
O MIGHTY ZEUS! BRING US VICTORY IN OUR HOUR OF NEED!
ZEUS HEARS YOU NOT, MY NOBLE FATHER. ALL IS LOST.
I GUESS THIS ISN'T THE TIME FOR I-TOLD-YOU-SO'S, BUT I DID!
PREPARE TO DIE, OLD FOOL!

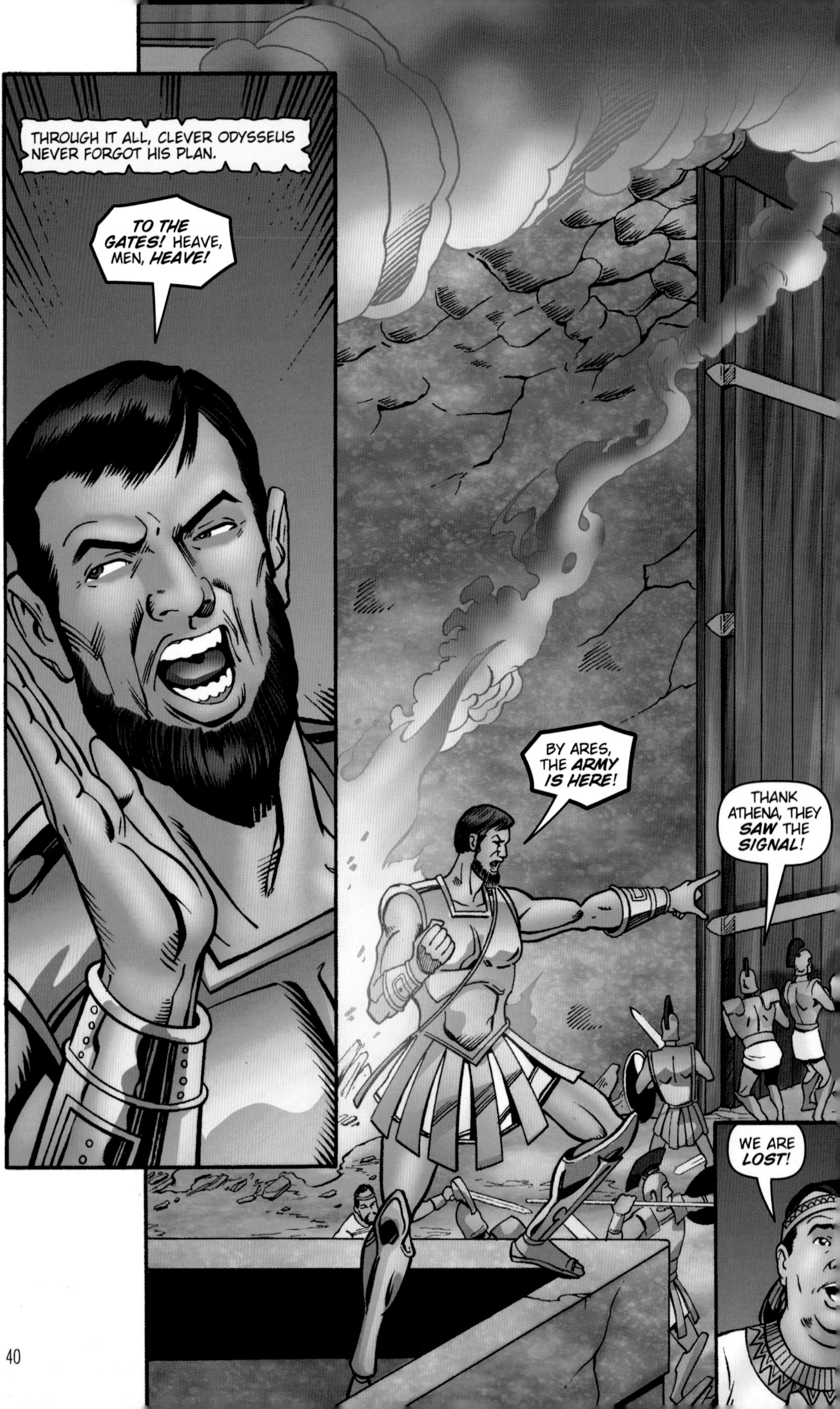
THROUGH IT ALL, CLEVER ODYSSEUS NEVER FORGOT HIS PLAN.
TO THE GATES! HEAVE, MEN, HEAVE!
BY ARES, THE ARMY IS HERE!
THANK ATHENA, THEY SAW THE SIGNAL!
WE ARE LOST!

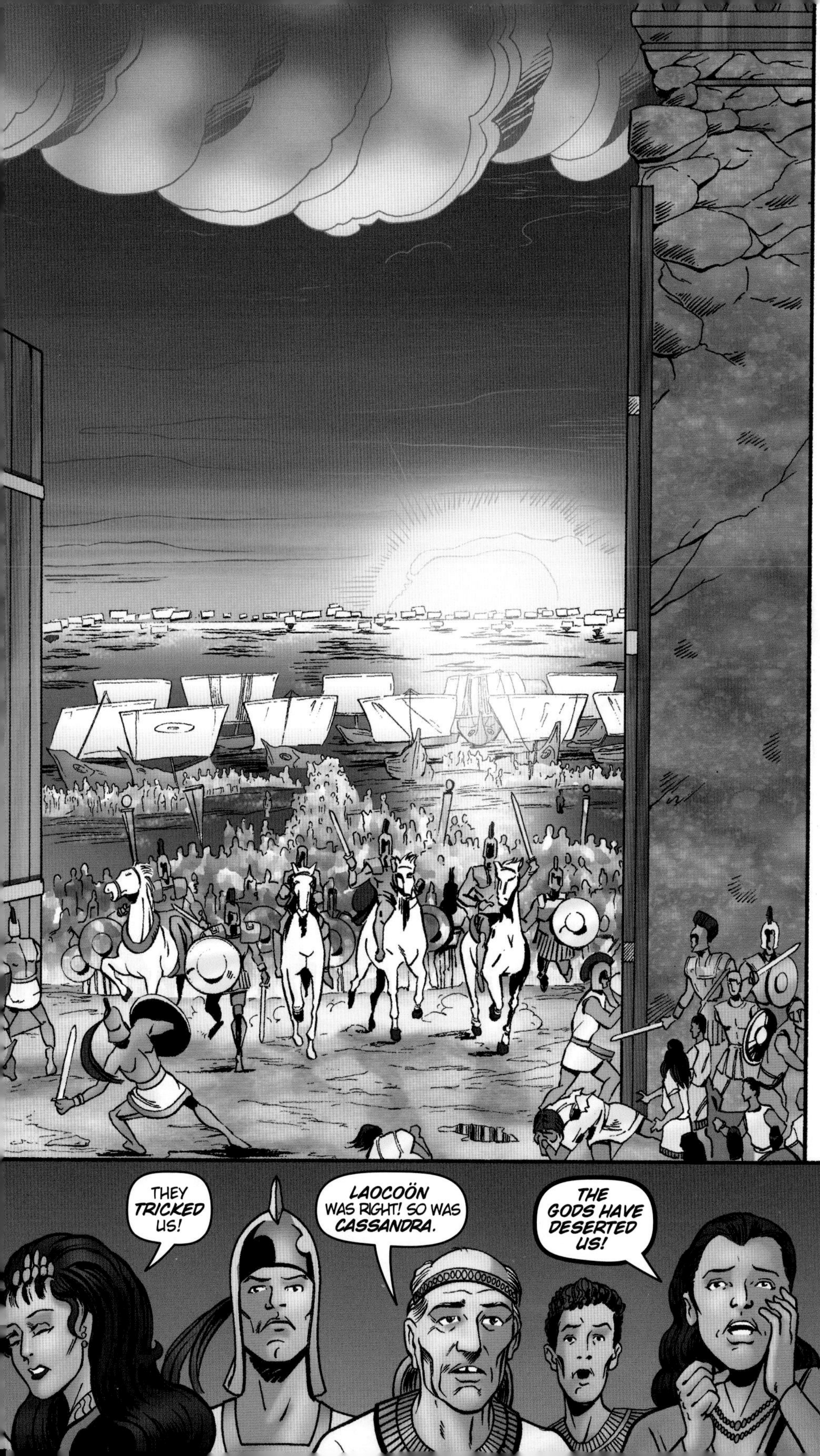
THEY TRICKED US!
LAOCOÖN WAS RIGHT! SO WAS CASSANDRA.
THE GODS HAVE DESERTED US!

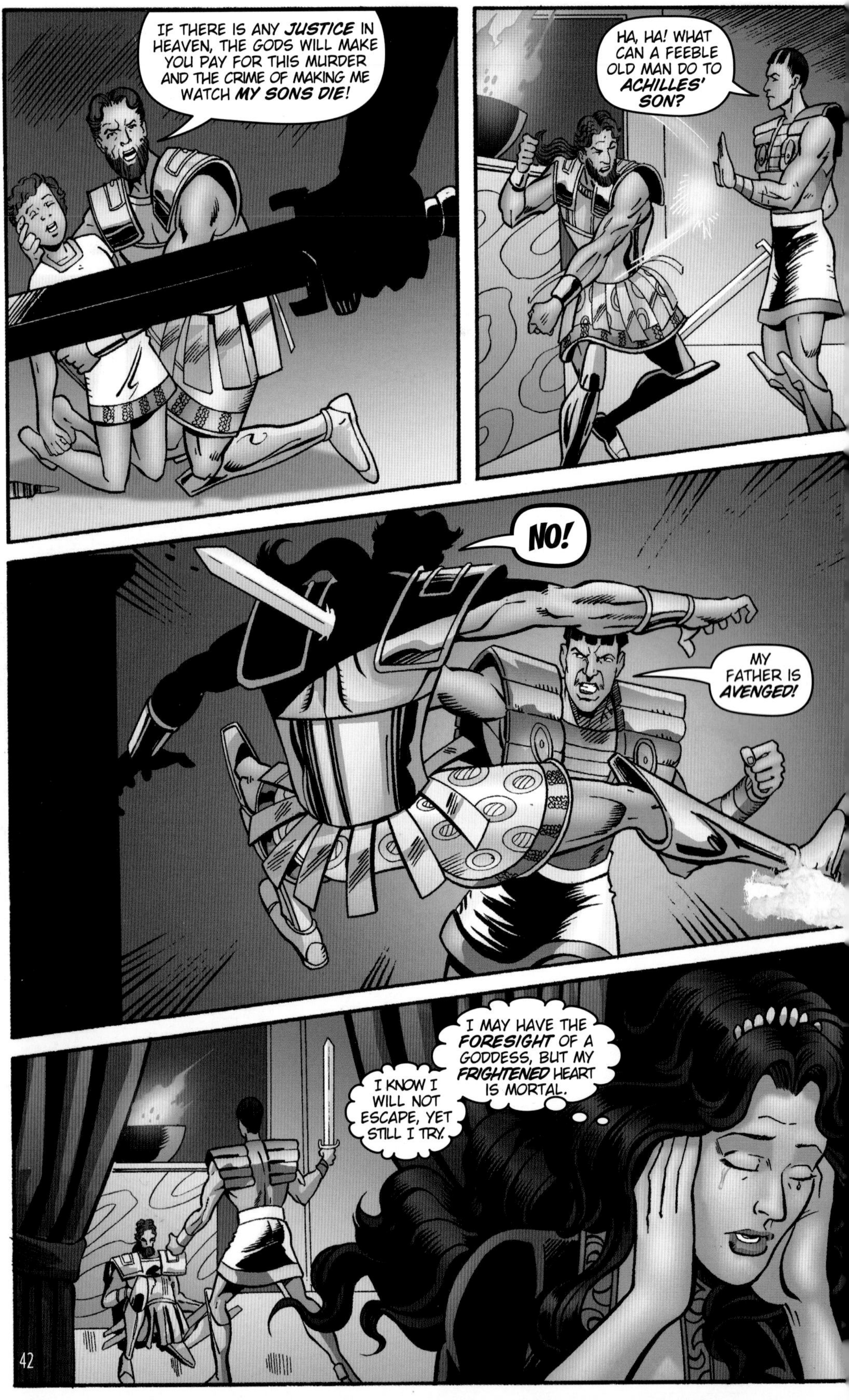
IF THERE IS ANY JUSTICE IN HEAVEN, THE GODS WILL MAKE YOU PAY FOR THIS MURDER AND THE CRIME OF MAKING ME WATCH MY SONS DIE!
HA, HA! WHAT CAN A FEEBLE OLD MAN DO TO ACHILLES' SON?
NO!
MY FATHER IS AVENGED!
I MAY HAVE THE FORESIGHT OF A GODDESS, BUT MY FRIGHTENED HEART IS MORTAL.
I KNOW I WILL NOT ESCAPE, YET STILL I TRY.

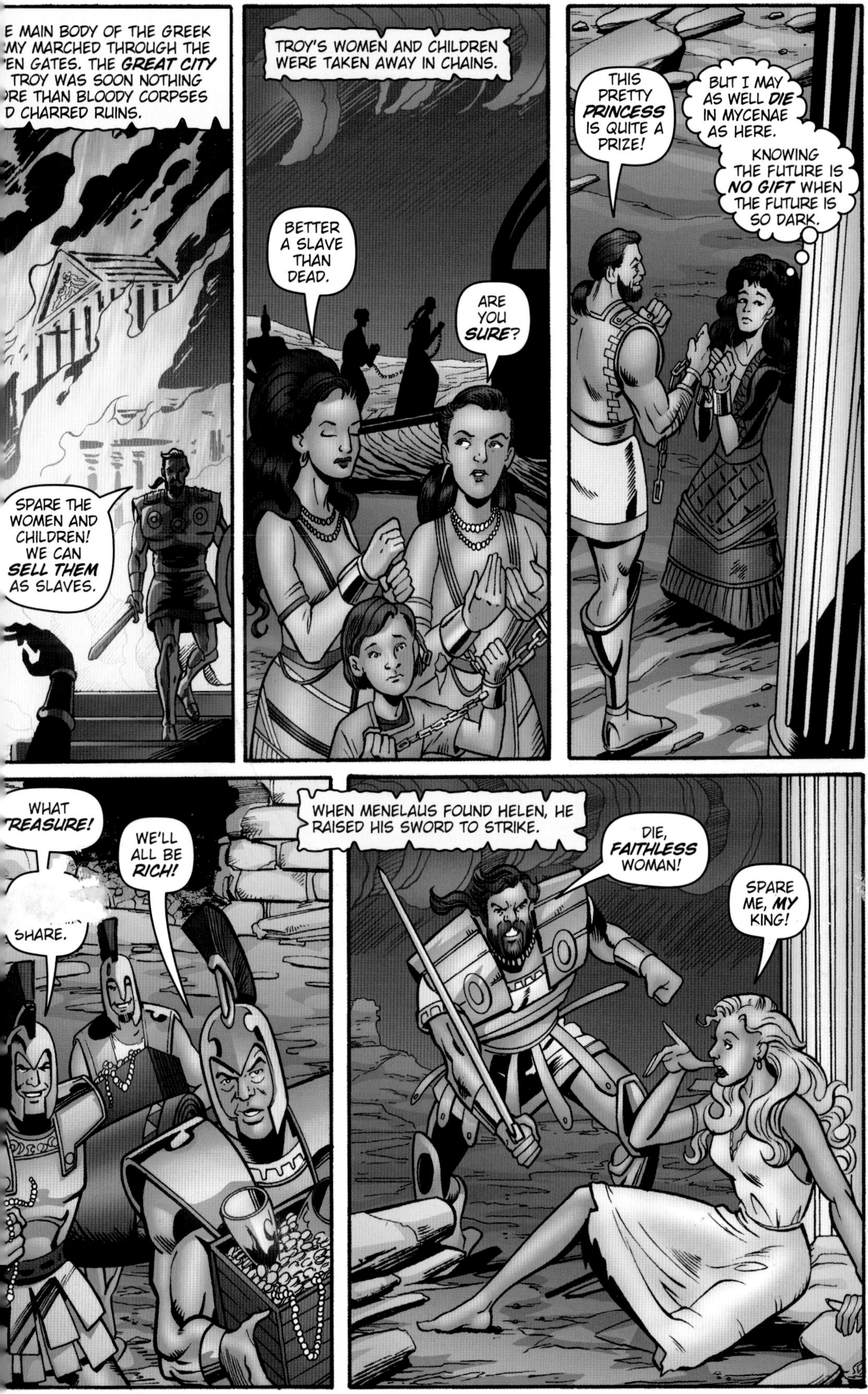
E MAIN BODY OF THE GREEK
MY MARCHED THROUGH THE
'EN GATES. THE GREAT CITY
TROY WAS SOON NOTHING
ORE THAN BLOODY CORPSES
D CHARRED RUINS.
SPARE THE WOMEN AND CHILDREN! WE CAN SELL THEM AS SLAVES.
TROY'S WOMEN AND CHILDREN WERE TAKEN AWAY IN CHAINS.
BETTER A SLAVE THAN DEAD.
ARE YOU SURE?
THIS PRETTY PRINCESS IS QUITE A PRIZE!
BUT I MAY AS WELL DIE IN MYCENAE AS HERE.
KNOWING THE FUTURE IS NO GIFT WHEN THE FUTURE IS SO DARK.
WHAT TREASURE!
SHARE.
WE'LL ALL BE RICH!
WHEN MENELAUS FOUND HELEN, HE RAISED HIS SWORD TO STRIKE.
DIE, FAITHLESS WOMAN!
SPARE ME, MY KING!

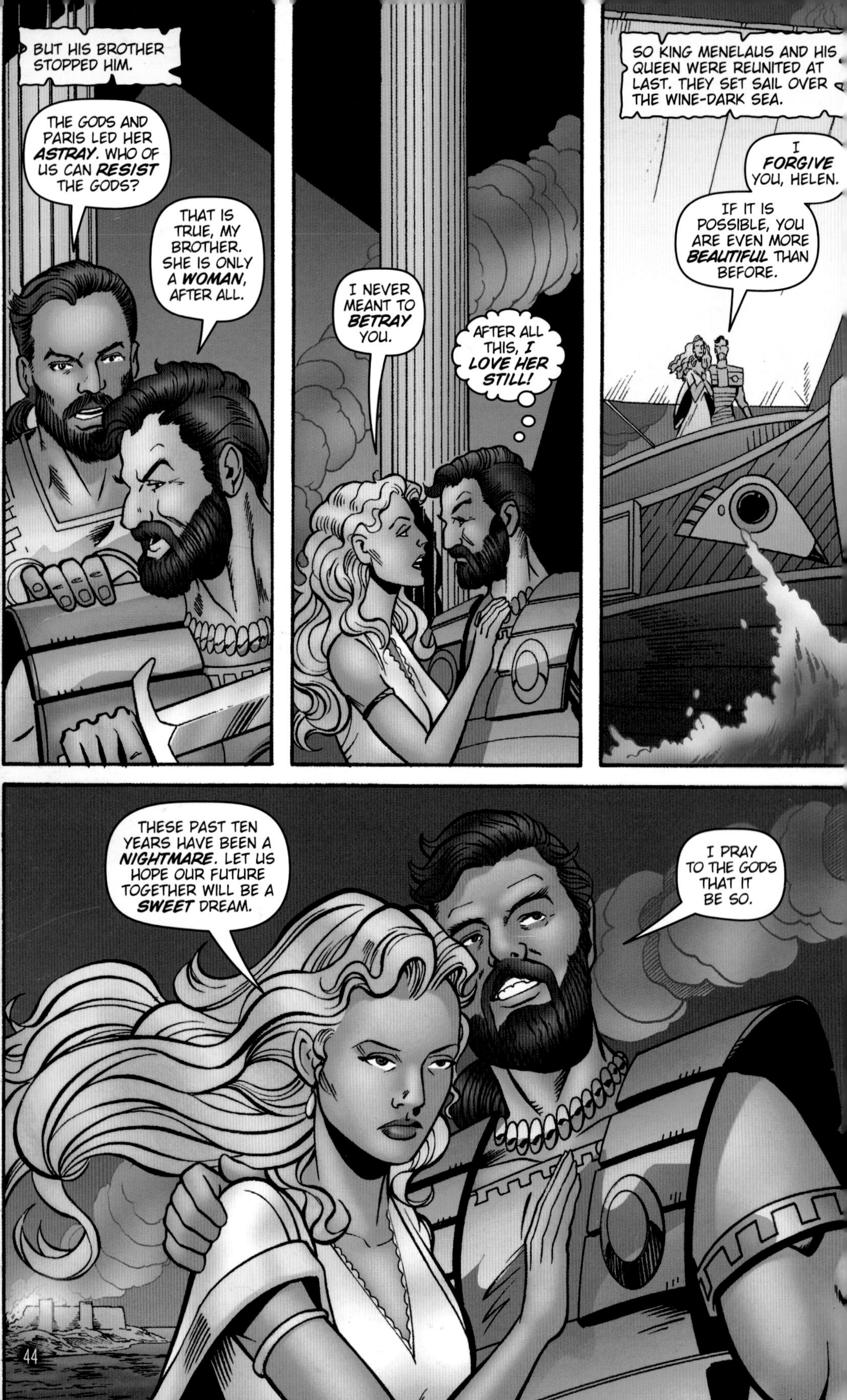
BUT HIS BROTHER STOPPED HIM.
THE GODS AND PARIS LED HER ASTRAY. WHO OF US CAN RESIST THE GODS?
THAT IS TRUE, MY BROTHER. SHE IS ONLY A WOMAN, AFTER ALL.
I NEVER MEANT TO BETRAY YOU.
AFTER ALL THIS, I LOVE HER STILL!
SO KING MENELAUS AND HIS QUEEN WERE REUNITED AT LAST. THEY SET SAIL OVER THE WINE-DARK SEA.
I FORGIVE YOU, HELEN.
IF IT IS POSSIBLE, YOU ARE EVEN MORE BEAUTIFUL THAN BEFORE.
THESE PAST TEN YEARS HAVE BEEN A NIGHTMARE. LET US HOPE OUR FUTURE TOGETHER WILL BE A SWEET DREAM.
I PRAY TO THE GODS THAT IT BE SO.

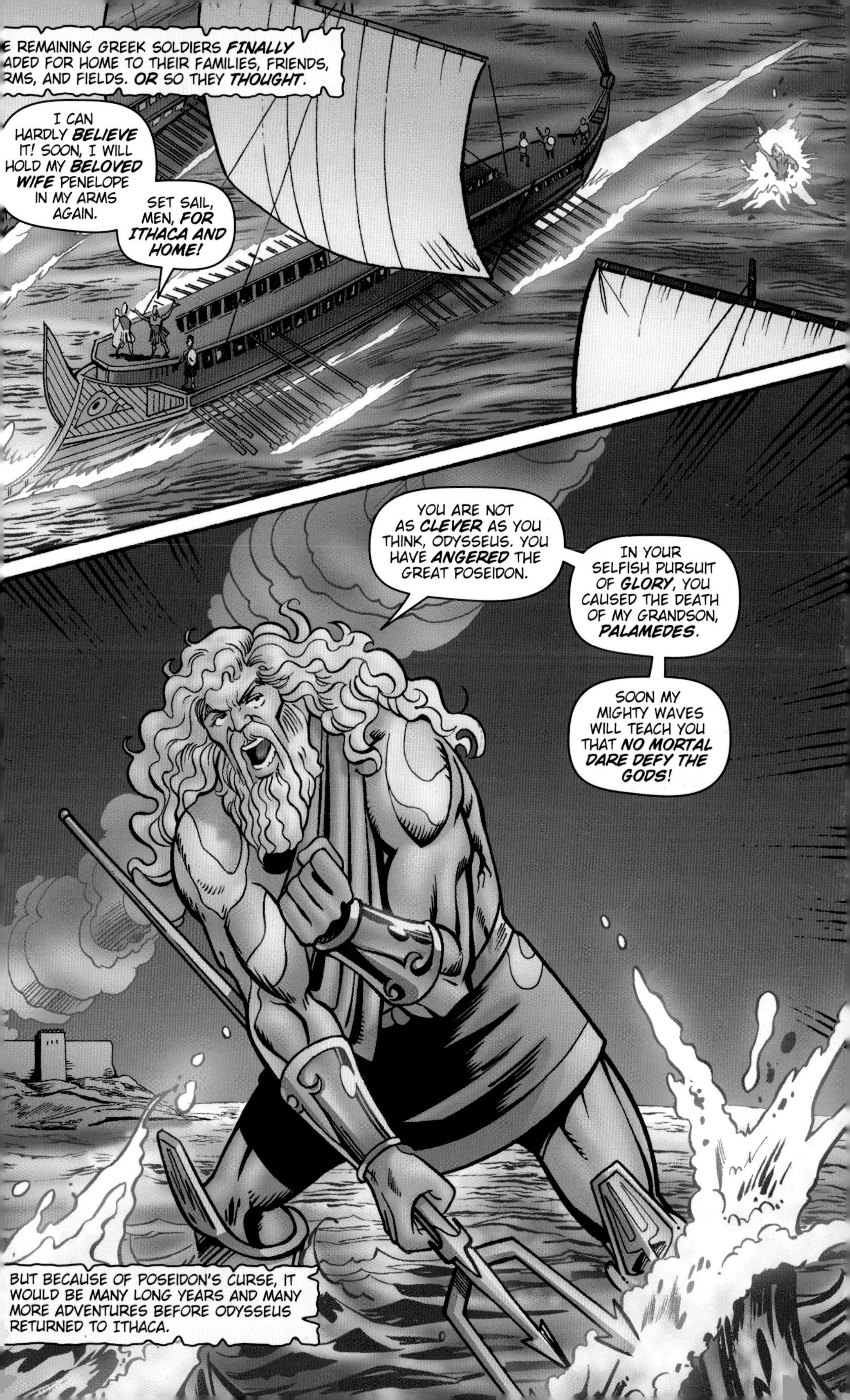

E REMAINING GREEK SOLDIERS FINALLY ADED FOR HOME TO THEIR FAMILIES, FRIENDS, RMS, AND FIELDS. OR SO THEY THOUGHT.
I CAN HARDLY BELIEVE IT! SOON, I WILL HOLD MY BELOVED WIFE PENELOPE IN MY ARMS AGAIN.
SET SAIL, MEN, FOR ITHACA AND HOME!
YOU ARE NOT AS CLEVER AS YOU THINK, ODYSSEUS. YOU HAVE ANGERED THE GREAT POSEIDON.
IN YOUR SELFISH PURSUIT OF GLORY, YOU CAUSED THE DEATH OF MY GRANDSON, PALAMEDES.
SOON MY MIGHTY WAVES WILL TEACH YOU THAT NO MORTAL DARE DEFY THE GODS!
BUT BECAUSE OF POSEIDON'S CURSE, IT WOULD BE MANY LONG YEARS AND MANY MORE ADVENTURES BEFORE ODYSSEUS RETURNED TO ITHACA.

GLOSSARY AND PRONUNCIATION GUIDE

ACHILLES (uh-*kil*-eez): son of Peleus and Thetis; prince of Phthia and Greek hero

AGAMEMNON (a-ga-*mem*-non): king of Mycenae; high king of the Achaeans

AJAX (*ay*-jax): Greek hero

APHRODITE (a-fro-*dye*-tee): goddess of love

APOLLO (uh-*pol*-oh): god of prophesy, music, and healing

ARES (*air*-eez): the god of war

ATHENA (uh-*thee*-nuh): goddess of wisdom

CASSANDRA (kuh-*san*-druh): daughter of King Priam and Queen Hecuba

ERIS (*ee*-ris): the goddess of discord

HADES (*hay*-deez): god of the dead

HECUBA (*hek*-yoo-buh): wife of King Priam

HELEN (*hell*-en): wife of King Menelaus

HERA (*hehr*-ruh): queen of the gods; goddess of the hearth

LAOCOÖN (lay-*uh*-koh-uhn): priest of Poseidon. He was killed by serpents after warning Troy to destroy the Trojan horse.

MENELAUS (meh-neh-*lay*-uhs): king; brother of Agamemnon

NEOPTOLEMUS (nee-op-*to*-leh-muhs): son of Achilles

ODYSSEUS (o-*dis*-see-uhs): king of Ithaca

PALAMEDES (pa-luh-*mee*-deez): prince of Nauplia; cousin of Agamemnon

PARIS (*pa*-ris): son of King Priam and Queen Hecuba

PENELOPE (pe-*nel*-oh-pee): wife of Odysseus

POSEIDON (po-*seye*-duhn): god of the ocean and earthquakes

PRIAM (*preye*-am): king of Troy

SINON (*si*-non): Greek spy who deceived Troy into bringing the Trojan horse into the city

ZEUS (*zyoos*): king of the gods; god of thunder and the sky

ink from pages 6-7

46

FURTHER READING AND WEBSITES

d'Aulaire, Ingri, and Edgar Parin d'Aulaire. *Book of Greek Myths*. New York: Dell Publishing, 1992.

Evslin, Bernard. *The Trojan War*. New York: Scholastic Book Services, 1971.

Fleischman, Paul. *Dateline, Troy*. Cambridge, MA: Candlewick Press, 1996.

Greek Myths—History for Kids
http://www.historyforkids.org/learn/greeks/religion/greekrelig.htm
This site provides information about Greek gods, heroes, and myths, as well as information about the Trojan War. It also includes links to related characters, websites, and books located in other websites.

Green, Roger Lancelyn. *The Tale of Troy: Retold from the Ancient Authors*. Baltimore: Puffin Books, 1958.

Hovey, Kate. *Voices of the Trojan War*. New York: Margaret K. McElderry Books, 2004.

McLaren, Clemence. *Inside the Walls of Troy: A Novel of the Women Who Lived the Trojan War*. New York: Atheneum, 1996.

Mythweb
http://www.mythweb.com/gods/index.html
This is an informative site about gods, heroes, and others. It also includes a link to the website's *Encyclopedia of Greek Mythology*.

Sutcliffe, Rosemary. *Black Ships Before Troy: The Story of the Iliad*. New York: Delacorte Press, 1993.

CREATING *THE TROJAN HORSE*

Ancient legends of a war between the Greek city states and Troy that may have taken place around 1200 B.C. were gathered into great epic poems by writers of later times. The Greek poet Homer wrote *The Iliad* about 700–800 B.C. It tells of the Greek heroes, particularly Achilles, as they fought against Troy to reclaim Helen, wife of Menelaus, king of Sparta. The story of the fall of Troy and of the horse left behind by the Greeks appears in the *Aeneid*, written by the Roman poet Virgil between 42 and 35 B.C. Ron & Justine Fontes have based their retelling on these sources and on *The War at Troy*, written by the Greek poet Quintus of Smyrna around A.D. 375.

INDEX

ABOUT THE AUTHORS AND ARTIST

RON & JUSTINE FONTES met at a publishing house in New York City. Ron worked for the comic book department, and Justine was an editorial assistant in children's books. Together they have written nearly 500 children's books, in every format from board books to historical novels.

From their home in Maine, the Fonteses publish *critter news*, a strictly-for-fun newsletter. They also launched Sonic Comics with their first graphic novel, *Tales of a Terminal Diner*, a unique anthology with continuing characters. Other published projects include *The Trojan Horse: The Fall of Troy* and *The Wooden Sword*. Life-long library lovers, the Fonteses long to write 1,1001 books before retiring.

GORDON PURCELL has had an extensive comic career, with credits including five different crews of StarTrek, The X-Files, Silver Sable, Superman, JLA, Robin, Aquaman, Flash, Wonder Man, Avengers, Lost in Space, Soulsearchers, and Xena. He's currently drawing issues of Flare for Heroic, Justice League Unlimited for DC, as well as biography comics. He lives in the frozen tundra of Minnesota with wife, Debra, and son, Jack.